BRANDENBURG GATE
The enduring symbol of Berlin. See page 52.

SANSSOUCI
Stroll around the palace gardens. See page 81.

SCHLOSS CHARLOTTENBURG
A baroque and rococo masterpiece. See page 69.

THE PERGAMONMUSEUM
See awe-inspiring wonders of the ancient world. See page 62.

NEUE NATIONALGALERIE
Explore the outstanding collection of 20th-century art. See page 47.

JEWISH MUSEUM
Tragic history and moving stories. See page 56.

CONTENTS

⊙ Walking Eye App

Your Insight Pocket Guide purchase includes a free download of the destination's corresponding eBook. It is available now from the free Walking Eye container app in the App Store and Google Play. Simply download the Walking Eye container app to access the eBook dedicated to your purchased book. The app also features free information on local events taking place and activities you can enjoy during your stay, with the option to book them. In addition, premium content for a wide range of other destinations is available to purchase in-app.

HOW TO DOWNLOAD THE WALKING EYE APP

Available on purchase of this guide only.
1. Visit our website: www.insightguides.com/walkingeye
2. Download the Walking Eye container app to your smartphone (this will give you access to your free eBook and the ability to purchase other products)
3. Select the scanning module in the Walking Eye container app
4. Scan the QR Code on this page – you will be asked to enter a verification word from the book as proof of purchase
5. Download your free eBook* for travel information on the go

* Other destination apps and eBooks are available for purchase separately or are free with the purchase of the Insight Guide book

INTRODUCTION

It's not much of an exaggeration to say that few cities in Europe evoke the continent's modern history more than Berlin. Almost everywhere you look stand reminders of the dramatic events of the 20th century, for Berlin is a city that publicly acknowledges its past – good and bad – through museums, memorials, and the preservation of historically significant buildings. At times, this can feel almost over-whelmingly poignant. Yet the vigour with which Berliners embrace the future, and their determination to move forward positively while showing respect for the suffering of the past, is truly inspiring. A visit to this lively, sophisticated city, which has borne witness to such extremes of human emotion, is an experience that lovers of history and travel alike will not forget in a hurry.

Germany's capital has excited pride for its strength, admiration for its culture, hatred as the centre of Hitler's tyranny, compassion as a bastion of post-war freedom, and fear as a focus of Cold War conflict. More than any other European capital, Berlin symbolises the immense changes wrought over the last century in Western and Eastern Europe.

For each emotion that the name Berlin evokes, the city has an appropriate symbol. The noble Schloss Charlottenburg and the monuments on Unter den Linden honour Germany's formidable Prussian past, while the Brandenburg Gate proclaims the city's regained unity. The Reichstag recalls united Germany's return to parliamentary democracy, while the gigantic Olympic Stadium expresses the bombast of Hitler's dictatorship. The chaos and destruction that the Nazis wrought find their deliberate reminder in the bombed-out shell of the Kaiser Wilhelm Memorial Church, while the atrocities of the Holocaust are represented by innumerable memorials big and small. The determination of the Jewish community to forge a stronger identity is best captured by the restored magnificence of the Neue Synagogue.

RELICS OF THE OLD DIVIDE

The eastern districts of the city – Mitte, Pankow, Friedrich-shain and Prenzlauer Berg – essentially form the old densely populated centre whose tenements (disparagingly referred to as *Mietskasernen*, literally meaning 'rental barracks') inspired the 1920s proletarian theatre of Erwin Piscator and Bertolt Brecht. When Berlin was divided up at the end of World War II, it seemed appropriate that the Soviet sector devoted to the Communist experiment should take in a large number of the working-class areas, while West Berlin had at its centre the eminently bourgeois neighbourhood of Charlottenburg.

OSTALGIE

As the film *Goodbye Lenin!* (2003) illustrates, there are some East Germans for whom reunification proved simply too much of a shock. Others may have accepted the demise of the GDR, but still look back wistfully on an era that did much good, despite the Communist dictatorship. In their nostalgia for the east (hence the term *Ostalgie*) people hanker for old certainties like jobs for life and workplace kindergartens. Basic items such as food and household products from the GDR are also high on the list. *Ostprodukte* are back in, just like icons that never even left, such as the red-and-green stop/go men, the *Ampelmännchen*, and that most enduring of children's TV characters, the *Sandmännchen*.

A rather different view of the GDR is presented in the book *Stasiland* by Anna Funder and the superb film *The Lives of Others* (2006), both of which examine the impact of state intrusion on personal life.

With reunification, two sets of people with different psychologies, economies and social systems were suddenly thrust together. Hitherto unforeseen problems emerged. As tens of thousands of East Germans came to settle in the West, entitling them to 'adjustment' money, housing subsidies and job retraining from the Bonn government, the financial burden of reunification now began to trouble West Germans, while a small minority of disgruntled West Berliners even began to wish that the Wall had never come down.

Friedrichstraße S-Bahn station

For the inhabitants of East Berlin, the merger with the West was not that idyllic either. The sudden impact of the West's free-market economy was in some cases disastrous, with some losing such benefits as controlled rents and job security. In former West German Chancellor Willy Brandt's immortal words, it is taking a long time, plus an enormous ongoing investment, for 'what belongs together to grow together'.

RECONSTRUCTION AND RENEWAL

The collapse of the Wall and the integration of two independent cities led to a flowering of culture. With no fewer than three opera houses, three major symphony orchestras and two national art galleries, Berlin is justifiably proud of its renewed artistic vigour. The Kulturforum in the Tiergarten was expanded, the magnificent Museumsinsel in the middle of the River Spree was restored, and major new museums such as the Jüdisches Museum opened their doors. Western Berlin's Schaubühne, along with the Berliner Ensemble, Volksbühne and Deutsches Theater from the East, now make up one of the world's most formidable theatrical establishments, promoting both classical tradition and the avant-garde. With the Berlin Film Festival as its flagship, cinema is resuming the excitement of its great creative period in the 1920s, a time commemorated in the exciting Film Museum Berlin (see page 48).

Some cynical Berliners claim that their city was transformed into Europe's largest building site, but the construction yielded office, retail and living space to accommodate a growing population that was boosted by the transfer of government

Queuing for the Reichstag

ministers and civil servants from Bonn to Berlin. Some of the buildings are remarkably beautiful, and the city almost feels like a living art gallery. The Reichstag, once more the seat of unified Germany's parliament, was topped with a huge glass dome, which is supposed to represent the lack of secrecy in modern German government. Daimler-Chrysler and Sony brought about a quite extraordinary transformation of Potsdamer Platz, and

Reflecting at the Kulturforum

shops, offices and apartments rose from the former Checkpoint Charlie. Gleaming shopping malls full of designer stores were constructed around Friedrichstraße, and old, dilapidated buildings in the east of the city were transformed into art galleries, exclusive fashion boutiques and trendy cafés. A particular hotspot of this kind is Scheunenviertel, north of Hackescher Markt S-Bahn station, where all signs of former economic deprivation have vanished.

BREATHING SPACE

Despite its stone, steel and glass, Berlin is the greenest metropolis in Europe, with almost 40 percent of its area occupied by lakes and rivers, parkland and woods. Besides the Tiergarten and the River Spree in the city centre, the southwest suburbs have the forest of the Grunewald, the River Havel and the Wannsee, while the north has the Tegel forest and lake. Small garden colonies abound, with flourishing farming communities, such as Lübars, set inside the city boundaries. To all of this, eastern Berlin adds its own Großer Müggelsee as well as the woods and parkland around Treptow and Köpenick.

There are more delightful excursions to be had beyond the city limits. Potsdam, at the other end of the Glienicke Bridge, lies within easy reach for a visit to Frederick the Great's Sanssouci Palace, with its extensive grounds. Alternatively, you could go walking in the surrounding forests and parks of Charlottenhof, Petzow and Werder, try a spot of boating on the Templiner Lake, or even make a pilgrimage to the monastery of Lehnin near Brandenburg.

YOUNG AT HEART

Beyond sightseeing, the most fascinating thing about Berlin is its people. Throughout the city's turbulent history, the individualism, courage and wit of Berliners have elicited the admiration of the watching world. A preconceived notion of Germans as a whole, but Prussians in particular, has often presented them as a cool and unfeeling people. However, such notions are quickly dispelled by the warmth and good humour exhibited by many of the city's people.

Younger Berlin's so-called 'alternative scene' has revived the city's 1920s reputation of lively and wildly independent-minded creativity, sometimes foundering in disillusioned nihilism in its strongholds, the working-class districts of Neukölln and Kreuzberg. Also to be found in these districts is Berlin's large community of immigrants, originally called *Gastarbeiter* ('guest workers'), most of them from Turkey, who add considerable colour and flavour to the city's social and gastronomic life.

This sprawling, invigorating metropolis attracts 11 million visitors a year, none of whom can help but feel a mixture of privilege and awe at witnessing such an exciting and evolving city.

A BRIEF HISTORY

Ironically, the German capital was already a divided city when it became a municipality during the 1200s. In those days the two rival halves were in no rush to unite. The fishermen of Cölln, whose name survives in the modern borough of Neukölln, lived on an island in the River Spree. The townships that comprise the modern Mitte district grew up around market places over which the people's churches, the Nikolaikirche and Marienkirche, still tower today. With the fortress of Burg Köpenick providing a common defence to the south, Cölln and Berlin formed a trade centre between Magdeburg and Poznan.

The hub of Old Berlin around the Nikolaikirche

In a region once inhabited by Slavic tribes, the population of the city was overwhelmingly German by the 13th century, consisting of enterprising merchants hailing from the northern Rhineland, Westphalia and Lower Saxony, with latecomers from Thuringia and the Harz. Berlin and Cölln came together in 1307 to lead the Brandenburg region's defences and defeat the robber barons who were terrorising merchants and local peasants. The prosperous city joined the Hanseatic League, trading in rye, wool and oak timber and providing an *entrepôt* for skins and furs from Eastern Europe.

Berlin continued as a virtually autonomous outpost of the German empire until 1448, when Brandenburg's Kurfürst (Prince Elector) Friedrich II took over control of the city after crushing the citizens' violent resistance, the so-called *Berliner Unwillen*. He was a member of the Hohenzollern dynasty that was to hold sway here for over 450 years.

The independent spirit of the Berliners was felt during the Reformation in the 16th century. The people were tired of paying the tribute exacted by the Catholic Church. In 1539, at a time when citizens of the other German principalities had to observe the religion of their prince, Berliners were successful in pressuring Prince Elector Joachim II to accept the Protestant creed as preached by Martin Luther.

Like the rest of Germany, the city was devastated by the Thirty Years' War (1618–48). Its Brandenburg rulers tried to befriend both the Protestant and Catholic armies but made enemies of both, leaving unfortified Berlin to pay the price.

PRUSSIA AND NAPOLEON

With his ambition of uniting the states of Brandenburg and Prussia, it was the Great Elector Friedrich Wilhelm (1640–88) who prepared Berlin to become a strong capital, and fortified it as a garrison town. The first newcomers were 50 wealthy Jewish families who had been expelled from Vienna in 1671. Then 14 years later 5,600 Huguenot Protestants arrived after being driven out of France by the revocation of the Edict of Nantes. At a time when France was considered the cultural master of Europe, these sophisticated merchants and highly skilled craftsmen – among them jewellers, tailors, chefs and

The easy life

Apparently living was easy in the 15th century, as historian Trithemius noted: 'Life here consists of nothing but eating and drinking.'

restaurant owners – brought a new refinement to the town.

This was further enhanced by the Great Elector's son who, in 1701, crowned himself in Königsberg (now Kaliningrad) King Friedrich in (not *of*) Prussia. Prompted by Sophie Charlotte, his wife, the king founded academies for the arts and sciences in Berlin. Baroque master Andreas Schlüter (see page 60) was commissioned to redesign the royal palace. This was knocked down in 1950 to make way for East Germany's Palast der Republik (demolished in 2008). Sophie Charlotte's

Schloss Charlottenburg

residence, however, the grand Schloss Charlottenburg, has been restored as a model of the era's elegance.

Friedrich Wilhelm I (1713–1740) despised the baroque glitter of his parents' court, and subjected the previously easy-going Berliners to a frugal, rigid concept of *Preussentum* (Prussianness), that is, unquestioning obedience to the ruler and his administrators, and sharply defined class distinctions, affirming the supremacy of the aristocracy, officer class and soldiers over civilians in general. An English cousin referred to Friedrich Wilhelm I as 'my brother the Sergeant', and the nickname stuck. The Soldier King spent his life in uniform and his courtiers followed suit. He had two obsessions: corporal punishment for the troops and washing his hands wherever he went. Irascible and deeply religious, he was simple in his personal tastes, finding the greatest pleasure in strictly male company over a pipe and a tankard of beer – wine struck him as too expensive.

Friedrich der Große (Frederick the Great, 1740–86), King *of* (not just *in*) Prussia, took his realm to the forefront of European politics and had little time for Berlin. He concentrated on turning his beloved Potsdam into a mini-Versailles, where French was spoken and Voltaire became his official philosopher-in-residence. He rarely appeared in Berlin except to garner public support – and taxes – after his return from costly wars with the Silesians, Russians and Austrians. He did, nevertheless, leave the German capital an enduring legacy with the monumental Forum Fridericianum laid out on Unter den Linden by his architect von Knobelsdorff.

The armies of Frederick's successors proved to be no match for Napoleon's Grande Armée, however, and as the French advanced through eastern Germany in 1806, Berlin's bureaucracy, court and bourgeoisie fled to the country. No troops were left to defend the city from its invaders, and Napoleon's march through the Brandenburg Gate into Berlin kindled a new flame of German patriotism.

ALL THE KING'S CABBAGES

When Friedrich Wilhelm I came to the throne, a wag's graffiti on the palace wall pinpointed the costs of his parents' extravagance: 'This castle is for rent and the royal residence of Berlin for sale.' To pay off the debts, he cut court officials' salaries from 250,000 silver thalers to 50,000, sold the opulent coronation robes, melted down the palace silver, and tore the flowers out of the Schloss Charlottenburg Park and replaced them with a far more practical crop: cabbages.

CAPITAL OF GERMANY

Defying the two years of French occupation, philosopher Johann Gottlieb Fichte exhorted the German people to assume their rightful destiny as a nation. Drummers were ordered to drown out his fiery speeches at the Royal Academy.

Frederick the Great

One of the uniting forces for the nationalist movement after the defeat of Napoleon were the *Lesecafés* (reading cafés) such as Spargnapani and Kranzler. They were a rendezvous for the intelligentsia who met to read foreign and provincial newspapers and glean information withheld in the heavily censored Berlin press.

Meanwhile, the accelerating industrial revolution had produced a new Berlin proletariat of 50,000 workers. Demonstrations were held to protest against working and living conditions, but they were crushed by the Prussian cavalry, leaving 230 dead. The king made small concessions, paying lip service to the demand for press freedom. A year later, police controls had been tightened, press censorship resumed, and democratic meetings swarmed with government spies.

Prussia's success during the Franco-Prussian War (1870–71) placed it at the head of a new united Germany. Under Kaiser Wilhelm I and Chancellor Bismarck, Berlin became the *Reichshauptstadt* (capital of the empire). By 1880, amid the industrial expansion of the *Gründerzeit* (founding years), the city's population soared past the million mark. Berlin boomed as the centre of Germany's engineering industry.

After its period of rapid growth, the city began to assume its place as Germany's cultural, as well as political capital, with Berlin artist Max Liebermann and others challenging Munich's dominance of German painting. The Berlin Philharmonic gained international standing, attracting Tchaikovsky, Strauss and Grieg as guest composers, and in 1905, the Viennese director Max Reinhardt arrived to head the Deutsches Theater.

Among its scientists, Robert Koch won a Nobel prize for his discovery of the *Tuberculosis bacillus*, and Max Planck headed the new Kaiser Wilhelm Society for the Advancement of Science (later named the Max-Planck-Gesellschaft), with none other than Albert Einstein as director of the physics department.

WAR AND REVOLUTION

After years of opposition on social matters, Berliners solidly supported what proved to be the Hohenzollerns' last military gasp

Crowds sing the national anthem in 1914

– World War I. At the start of the hostilities in August 1914, people gathered in their thousands to cheer the Kaiser at the royal palace. The enthusiasm was short-lived.

Rosa's memorial

A memorial tablet by the Lichtenstein Bridge marks the spot where Rosa Luxemburg's body was thrown into the Landwehr Canal.

Privations at home and the horrendous loss of life on the front turned popular feeling against the war. In 1916, Karl Liebknecht and Rosa Luxemburg formed the Spartacus League. Two years later, with Germany defeated, revolution broke out in Berlin. While the Social Democrats were proclaiming a new German Republic, Liebknecht took over the palace, declaring the Republic socialist.

Vehemently opposed to any Soviet-style revolution, Chancellor Friedrich Ebert and his Social Democrats outmanoeuvred the Spartacists. Some 4,000 *Freikorps* (right-wing storm-troopers) were called in to smash the movement. They assassinated Liebknecht and Luxemburg on 15 January 1919. Four days later, a new National Assembly was elected and the dominant Social Democrats moved the government to the safety of Weimar to draw up the constitution of the new Republic.

The use of the *Freikorps* to suppress the Spartacists was to haunt the Weimar Republic. In March 1920, the Kapp Putsch brought 5,000 of the storm-troopers into Berlin with an obscure civil servant, Wolfgang Kapp, installed as puppet chancellor. The coup lasted only five days, but set the tone for Germany's fragile experiment in parliamentary democracy. The swastika displayed on the helmets of the *Freikorps* was to reappear on the armbands of Hitler's storm-troopers, crushing all democracy in 1933.

THE GOLDEN TWENTIES

The turbulent twenties gave Berlin a special place in the world's popular imagination. In 1920, the incorporation of eight townships and some 60 suburban communities into the metropolis effectively doubled Berlin's population overnight to four million. Before democracy was extinguished in 1933, the city led a charmed life of exciting creativity that left its mark on the whole of European culture. Defeat in World War I had shattered the rigid certainties of Berlin's 'Prussianness' and left the town open to radical adventures in social and artistic expression almost unimaginable in the older cultural capitals of Vienna, London and Paris.

Artists of the avant-garde intellectual movement known as Dada called for state prayers to be replaced by simultaneous poetry and regularisation of sexual intercourse via a Central Dada Sex Office. Many years before the New York 'happenings' of the 1960s, Berlin Dadaists were organising races between a sewing machine and a typewriter, with writer Walter Mehring and artist Georg Grosz as jockeys. In the meantime, nightclubs on Tauentzienstraße provided a combination of political satire and striptease, accompanied by copious amounts of alcohol, cocaine and sexual licence. The paintings of Otto Dix, Georg Grosz and Max Beckmann were brutally realist, and the dissonance of the times was aptly captured by the atonal music composed

FILM GREATS

Berlin showed its sense of the times with its mastery of film, the 20th-century art form. Fritz Lang, F.W. Murnau, G.W. Pabst and Ernst Lubitsch were the leading directors of their generation. While Hollywood had considered cinema to be principally an industry of mass entertainment, the Berlin film-makers added a new perception of its artistic possibilities with M, The Cabinet of Dr Caligari, Lulu and Nosferatu. After seeing Fritz Lang's premonitory fable of human regimentation, Metropolis, Hitler wanted the master of the dark spectacle to make publicity films for him.

by Arnold Schönberg and his pupil Alban Berg.

The conservative establishment winced when the Prussian Writers' Academy chose as its president Heinrich Mann, the elder brother of Thomas Mann, a violent critic of the bourgeoisie and a Communist Party supporter. His best-known novel, *Professor Unrat*, inspired Josef von Sternberg's *The Blue Angel*, the film that revealed the vocal talents of Marlene Dietrich.

Girls perform at a jazz concert

Berlin was going through a wild time, but the Versailles peace treaty had laid heavy burdens on the nation. At the start of the twenties, inflation had made a farce of the German currency, and political assassinations became routine. The most significant of the victims was foreign minister Walther Rathenau, an enlightened democrat and Jew who was murdered near the Grunewald forest. It was also the time of vicious street battles between Communists and Nazis, both exploiting the social disruptions of inflation and unemployment that were impossible to ignore.

THE THIRD REICH

Communist hostility towards the Social Democrats split the opposition to the Nazis. Hitler became Chancellor on 30 January 1933. Only a month later, on 27 February, the Reichstag went up in flames. Hitler used the fire as a pretext to eliminate Communist and all left-wing opposition from German political life. The Nazi reign of terror had begun.

Flames were the leitmotiv of the Third Reich in Berlin. On 10 May 1933, a procession brought thousands of students along

Unter den Linden to the square before Humboldt University. They carried books, not to a lecture but to a bonfire on which were burned the works of Thomas Mann, Heinrich Mann, Stefan Zweig, Albert Einstein and Sigmund Freud, as well as Proust, Zola, Gide, H.G. Wells and Jack London. In 1936 a flame was brought from Athens to Berlin to inaugurate the Olympic Games, an attempt at Aryan propaganda which was soundly subverted by black athlete Jesse Owens, who won four gold medals. In deference to foreign visitors, all anti-Semitic signs such as *Juden unerwünscht* (Jews not wanted) were removed from shops, hotels and cafés. As soon as the foreigners had left town, the signs went up again.

Discrimination against the Jews moved inexorably to the night of 9 November 1938, when synagogues and other Jewish-owned buildings were torched, and shops looted. This pogrom became known as *Kristallnacht*, 'the Night of Broken Glass'. Berlin's Jewish population, which stood at 170,000 in 1933, was reduced by emigration and extermination to around 6,000 by 1945.

WORLD WAR II

In the autumn of 1938, as Hitler's army was preparing to march into neighbouring Czechoslovakia, Berliners shared none of the fervour that had greeted military parades in 1914. Their disquiet was shortly to be justified. The first bombing raids came in 1940 from the British in retaliation for the air raids on London. Attacks were stepped up after the German defeat at Stalingrad in 1943, with Anglo-American 'carpet-bombing'. The worst single raid was on 6 February 1945, when bombs wiped out 4 sq km (1.5 sq miles) of the city centre in one hour. Hitler spent the last days of the war in his bunker at the Reich chancellery. As Soviet troops moved in to capture the city, he committed suicide with a shot through the mouth.

The war ended with unconditional German surrender on 8 May 1945. In Berlin, the population was left to pick up the pieces

– literally. Women formed groups of *Trümmerfrauen* (rubble women), with 60,000 of them passing the debris of war by hand to clear the ground for rebuilding.

DIVISION AND REUNIFICATION

With the Soviet army already in place, American troops entered Berlin in 1945 on their national Independence Day, 4 July, followed by the British and French contingents. Control of Berlin by the four powers was agreed at Potsdam by Winston Churchill, Harry Truman and Joseph Stalin. The Soviet eastern sector covered just under half the city's area; the French, British

Newly elected Chancellor Adolf Hitler in the Reichstag, May 1933

and Americans divided the western sector between them.

The Allies soon found themselves confronted with Soviet efforts to incorporate the whole of Berlin into a Communist-controlled eastern Germany. In the 1946 municipal elections – Berlin's first free vote since 1933, and its last until 1990 – the Social Democrats won a crushing victory over the Communists, prompting the Soviets to tighten their grip on the eastern sector. Unhappy that West Berlin's capitalist presence in the middle of East Germany was having a subversive influence on the Communist experiment, the Soviets and their East German allies began to restrict traffic from West Germany. In June 1948, all road, rail and waterway routes to West Berlin

US plane with supplies for Soviet-blockaded West Berlin, 1948

were sealed off. The Western Allies countered the blockade by airlifting into Berlin between 4,000 and 8,000 tons of food and other vital supplies every day for 11 months. The blockade ended in May 1949, and West Berlin became a *Land* linked administratively with the new Federal Republic of Germany, which had Bonn as its capital. East Berlin was made capital of the fledgling German Democratic Republic (GDR).

Discontent with living conditions in East Berlin first erupted into open revolt on 17 June 1953. Striking workers marched down Stalinallee (soon after renamed Karl-Marx-Allee) to demonstrate against the government of Walter Ulbricht. They were protesting against the state demands for increased productivity, while their standard of living continued to compare poorly with that of West Berlin. Soviet tanks crushed the revolt.

By the end of the 1950s, over 3 million citizens had fled East Germany in search of a better life, over half of them through Berlin. The authorities decided to put a stop to the haemorrhage. In the early hours of 13 August 1961, the East German military began to erect a wall that would separate East and West Berlin and change the lives of several million people for almost three decades. Masterminded by Ulbricht and Erich Honecker, the Berlin Wall grew from an improvised barbed-wire fence into a massive barrier close to 4m (13ft) high, topped by concrete tubing. Behind it, protected by an electrified fence, stretched a strip of sand 150m (160yds) wide – a no-man's land equipped with watch-towers, patrol dogs and searchlights. The most poignant stretch was in the district of Wedding, where Bernauer Straße ran one side in the east, the other in the west. After the border was closed in August 1961, people jumped to freedom from windows until workmen bricked them up.

For the Western Alliance, the Wall made West Berlin an even more powerful symbol of freedom. On his visit in 1963, US President John F. Kennedy dramatically underlined the Western Allies' commitment to the city with his famous proclamation: *'Ich bin ein Berliner.'*

Erich Honecker's regime won international diplomatic recognition for East Berlin as its capital and, with gleaming hotels and skyscrapers, tried to give it a certain lustre to rival West Berlin. Beneath the surface, however, the drabness of daily life and lack of personal freedom undermined any chance of popular support.

The final push that led to the collapse of the Berlin Wall came when an ecological campaign in Leipzig against nuclear weapons and industrial pollution grew into nationwide pressure for democratic freedom. In 1989, with thousands of East Germans fleeing to the West via Hungary, Czechoslovakia and Poland, the country was swept up in Eastern European revolutions fuelled by the reforms of Soviet leader Mikhail Gorbachev. His visit to East Berlin in October 1989 for the 40th anniversary

Break for freedom

Civilian escapes by tunnel, cars with hidden compartments, and other subterfuges, including by hot-air balloon, became as much a part of the Cold War legend as break-outs by prisoners of war in World War II.

of the GDR left it clear that Soviet troops would no longer prop up its regime. The Berlin Wall was opened on 9 November 1989, and at midnight on 3 October 1990, a huge black, red and gold national flag was hoisted at the Reichstag. East and West Berlin were united once more.

THE CITY TODAY

With a population of almost three and a half million, reunited Berlin was by far Germany's largest city and was quickly declared the national capital again. On 20 June 1991, the city's role at the hub of German life was assured when the Bundestag voted by a slim majority to restore Berlin as the seat of government. In May 1999 a federal President was elected at the Reichstag and, in August that year, government business was finally moved back from Bonn to Berlin.

Berlin continued its transformation in the early years of the 21st century. The new government quarter was completed, new foreign embassies were erected and old ones refurbished. Restoration of historic buildings proceeded apace, and the realisation of major new schemes such as at Potsdamer Platz made Berlin a showcase for modern urban design.

The latest additions to the city's architectural attractions are the giant Hauptbahnhof (Central Station) – an attractive glass palace built in 2006 close to the Kanzleramt (Federal Chancellery) – and the new Brandenburg airport, built to replace three airports serving the German capital, due to open in the second half of 2017. The Stadtschloss, Berlin's old royal and imperial palace, on the site of the demolished East German Parliament, the Palast der Republik, is being rebuilt under a €590m (£500m) construction project with a view to opening to the public as a museum and hotel in 2019. Berlin has fared relatively well during the world economic downturn, though in 2015 it still lagged behind the cities of Germany's west.

HISTORICAL LANDMARKS

Beginnings
1237–44 First record of Cölln and Berlin.
1307 The two townships are consolidated as one city.
1486 Residence of the Elector of Brandenburg.
Reformation
1539 Berliners force Elector Joachim II to become a Protestant.
1618–48 Thirty Years' War and plague halve population to barely 5,000.
1696–1700 Arts and science academies founded.
Rise of Prussia
1740–86 Frederick the Great ascends the throne.
1791 Brandenburg Gate completed.
1848 Democratic revolt crushed.
Capital of Germany
1871 Bismarck makes Berlin capital of Germany.
1918 November Revolution; new Republic at the Reichstag.
1933 Hitler imposes a dictatorship after Reichstag fire.
1936 Berlin hosts XI Olympic Games.
1938 9 November: Kristallnacht pogrom.
1939–45 World War II cuts population in half.
Division and Unification
1945 Berlin is divided and controlled by the Four Powers (France, the Soviet Union, the USA and Great Britain).
1953 17 June: Soviet tanks crush East Berlin uprising.
1961 Construction of the Berlin Wall.
1989 East German regime toppled; Berlin Wall opened.
1990 Reunited Berlin elects its first unified parliament in over 40 years.
1991 Berlin again becomes the seat of government.
1999 The Bundestag commences business at the Reichstag.
2009 The Palast der Republik is demolished.
2013 US President Obama visits the city.
2014 Germany wins the FIFA World Cup over Argentina.
2015 The 25th anniversary of the reunification of Germany.

WHERE TO GO

You'll need to plan carefully for a thorough exploration of Berlin; with a total area of 880 sq km (340 sq miles) it is bigger than most European capitals. Since the reorganisation of the municipal transport system, virtually the whole of the city is accessible via underground (U-Bahn), district railways (S-Bahn), bus or tram. You should have no difficulty in reaching the outlying areas, including Grunewald and Potsdam, by public transport, which runs 24 hours a day. There is absolutely no need for a car in Berlin.

A good orientation exercise is to start with an organised sightseeing tour. Many bus tours depart from the eastern end of the Kurfürstendamm in west Berlin or from Alexanderplatz on the eastern side of the city and are hop-on/hop-off. Alternatively, cruises on the Landwehrkanal or Spree and Havel rivers offer a more leisurely way of taking in areas of eastern and western Berlin that are not normally covered by the tour buses.

This guide takes in the sights of Central Berlin from west to east, starting

> **Taking the S-Bahn**
>
> A good initial way of getting the measure of Berlin is to take the S-Bahn around the centre, from Zoologischer Garten to Alexanderplatz. From the elevated track you get impressive views of some major landmarks, including the Reichstag.

at the Kurfürstendamm, then on to the Tiergarten Area, and through the Brandenburg Gate to Unter den Linden. In the west, a tourist information centre can be found at Neues Kranzler Eck on Kurfürstendamm 22 and is open every day from 10am; the helpful staff will assist you with maps, leaflets and any questions you may have about your visit.

Berlin's Cathedral

AROUND THE KURFÜRSTENDAMM

West Berlin's main thoroughfare, literally 'Prince Elector's Embankment', is known to Berliners as the **Ku'damm ❶**. It extends for 3.5km (about 2 miles) through the western part of the city centre, forming a triangular area enclosed by Lietzenburger Straße, Hardenbergstraße, Leibnizstraße and Tauentzienstraße. Here you will find a vast array of shops, cafés, restaurants, theatres, cinemas and art galleries, as well as no-frills fast-food stands and the inevitable souvenir sellers.

Impressed by the prolongation of the Champs-Elysées in Paris to the Bois de Boulogne, Bismarck wanted to extend the Ku'damm out as far as the Grunewald forest. However, such pretentions were never realised, and finally the avenue linked Kaiser Wilhelm Memorial Church to nothing grander than the Halensee railway station.

Kurfürstendamm U-Bahn station

The avenue lost almost all the Jugendstil architecture of its Wilhelminian heyday during World War II, and only a few vestiges survive. Otherwise the street is resolutely modern – gleaming glass, steel and an occasional touch of marble – but still a magnet for fashion-conscious shoppers.

> **Literaturhaus**
>
> Next door to the Käthe-Kollwitz-Museum is the Literaturhaus, where readings, seminars and discussions are held. The villa is surrounded by a delightful garden, and there is a pleasant café, the Café Wintergarten.

KRANZLER ECK

Like so much of the city, this neighbourhood is in a constant state of redevelopment. The **Kranzler Eck** (Kranzler Corner), where the city's most stylish citizens once stopped off for coffee and cakes, has been transformed by the addition of a stunning 16-storey glass skyscraper, designed by Helmut Jahn of Chicago and completed in 2002. As well as offices, the City Quartier has shops and restaurants. The **Café Kranzler** is still there, but it no longer looks quite as dominant as it once did.

Off the Ku'damm at Fasanenstraße 79, you will find the **Jüdisches Gemeindezentrum** (Jewish Community Centre). Framing the entrance is the domed portal from the synagogue, which was burned during the fateful *Kristallnacht* ('Night of Broken Glass') of 1938 (see page 24). The modern building serves as a cultural centre for the 12,000 Jews living in Berlin today – in 1933 they numbered some 170,000.

At Fasanenstraße 24 stands the intimate **Käthe-Kollwitz-Museum** (www.kaethe-kollwitz.de; daily 11am–6pm; charge). On display is a comprehensive collection of sketches, drawings and sculptures by the artist Käthe Kollwitz (1867–1945), whose work resounds with compassion as she makes appeals on behalf of the working poor, the suffering and the sick.

It is worth exploring some of the other side streets off the Ku'damm. As well as Fasanenstraße, you will discover many other elegant tree-lined boulevards studded with beautiful, balconied villas, antiques shops, art galleries and exclusive designer boutiques. A little to the north, **Savignyplatz** provides a focus for first-class art and architecture bookshops and art galleries, located in the arches beneath the overhead S-Bahn railway line. Here you will find an abundance of literary cafés, bistros and bars, with plenty of outside seating.

BREITSCHEIDPLATZ

To the east of the Kranzler Eck, the Ku'damm leads through to **Breitscheidplatz**, a large pedestrianised area at the base of the Europa-Center and a busy gathering place for shoppers and sightseers during the day. In the centre of the square is Joachim Schmettau's granite **Weltkugelbrunnen** (or Fountain of the World), which locals have cheerily christened the Wasserklops ('aquatic meatball').

Soaring above it is an enduringly powerful symbol of the city, the **Kaiser-Wilhelm-Gedächtniskirche ❷** (Kaiser-Wilhelm Memorial Church; www.gedaechtniskirche-berlin.de; daily 9am–7pm). The 1943 bombing, combined with artillery fire at the end of the war, left the tower with the broken stump of its spire – 63m (206ft), compared with its original 113m (370ft) – as a monumental ruin recalling the city's destruction. Flanking it, a modern octagonal church to the east and a chapel and hexagonal tower to the west represent the city's post-war rebirth. Stained glass made in Chartres and set in walls of moulded concrete casts a mysterious bluish glow over the Ku'damm at night.

Built between 1891 and 1895 to honour Wilhelm I, the remains of this neo-Romanesque church constitute a memorial hall to celebrate the Hohenzollerns' pious monarchism. A

Christ the King mosaic in the Kaiser-Wilhelm Memorial Church

mosaic representing Christ the King is set above friezes and reliefs of Prussian monarchs from Friedrich I (1415–40) to the last crown prince, Friedrich Wilhelm. On one wall, Wilhelm I confers with Chancellor Bismarck and Field Marshals Moltke and Roon. With their taste for irreverent nicknames, Berliners have deflated the monuments' imperial or pacifist intentions by dubbing the original church the 'broken tooth' and the two main additions the 'lipstick' and 'powder compact'.

Beyond the church is the enormous **Europa-Center**, between Tauentzienstraße and Budapester Straße. The centre was built in the 1960s and houses scores of shops, restaurants, a hotel and a theatre amid artificial ponds and waterfalls. On the 20th floor, the PURO Sky Lounge nightclub and bar (www.puroberlin.de; Thur–Sat 8pm–3am) offers spectacular views over the city.

A multi-media experience in the Ku'damm Karree (Ku'damm 207–208) dramatically relates 800 years of the city's history. The frequent English-language tours relating **The Story of**

Berlin (daily 10am–8pm) include a visit to an underground nuclear bunker.

THE ZOO

Accessed from Budapester Straße, the **Zoo ❸** (www.zoo-berlin. de; daily Mar–Sept 9am–7pm, Oct 9am–6pm, Nov–Feb 9am–5pm; charge), is Germany's oldest (opened 1841) and has one of the most varied collections of animals in Europe. Beyond the pagoda-arched **Elefantentor** (Elephant Gate) are 35 hectares (86 acres) of parkland where you can observe Indian and African elephants, giant pandas and the rare Indian single-horned rhinoceros. This was also the home of the late hand-raised polar bear, Knut. Dating from 1913, the **Zoo-Aquarium Berlin** houses numerous species of fish and reptiles, and an impressive collection of arthropods.

Berlin sculpture, with the Europa-Center to the right

TAUENTZIENSTRASSE

From Breidscheidplatz, follow the double-laned **Tauentzienstraße** to the east. In the pleasantly landscaped central reservation, notice the intertwined steel tubes of the *Berlin* sculpture ❹, which was designed for the city's 750th anniversary in 1987. The two halves are tantalisingly close to each other, yet fail to touch, poignantly symbolising the once divided city.

WITTENBERGPLATZ

At the far end of Tauentzien-straße, **Wittenbergplatz** is a large, populous square and contains one of Berlin's many memorials: a stark sign outside the U-Bahn station which reminds passers-by of the Nazi concentration camps. The station itself is a

Elephant at the Zoo

beautifully restored Art Deco delight with lovely wooden ticket booths, period posters and a central standing clock.

More than just a department store, **KaDeWe** (Kaufhaus des Westens, www.kadewe.de), located on the edge of Wittenbergplatz, has become a monument since its foundation in 1907. The food emporium on the sixth floor is extraordinary. Here, gourmet globetrotters can perch on a bar stool and sample not only food from all over Germany but also Chinese, Japanese, Russian, French and Swiss cuisine. One floor up, the Wintergarten is a vast food court in the glass-roofed atrium where shoppers can help themselves to more scrumptious fare. It is an ideal spot for a hearty breakfast before a day's shopping. The fashion department (spread across three floors) is also well worth a visit.

TIERGARTEN AREA

Despite its name, the leafy **Tiergarten** (literally 'animal garden') is not another zoo. For the Hohenzollern princes it was a forest for hunting deer and wild boar. After Frederick the Great cut down the woods to create a formal French garden for his brother August Ferdinand, it was replanted with trees in the 19th century and transformed into a landscaped park. Following World War II, the Berliners stripped away the trees again, this time for fuel. Everything you see here has been planted since 1950, among pleasant ponds, cafés and various monuments.

Within the park, the **Englischer Garten** was laid out by the Shropshire Horticultural Society, and forms part of the grounds of the neoclassical **Schloss Bellevue**, official residence of the German President.

HANSAVIERTEL

On the northwest side of the Tiergarten is the **Hansaviertel**, a residential neighbourhood rebuilt by architects for the International Building Exhibition of 1957. Among the winners were Bauhaus founder Walter Gropius (Händelallee 1–9), the Brazilian Oscar Niemeyer (Altonaer Straße 4–14) and Alvar Aalto from Finland (Klopstockstraße 30). Their names are inscribed along with the locations of their projects on a map on Klopstockstraße. Nearby, at Hanseatenweg 10, the **Akademie der Künste** (Arts Academy), distinguished by the splendid Henry Moore sculpture outside, holds concerts, plays and exhibitions of avant-garde art.

SIEGESSÄULE

At the centre of the park, on the circle of the Großer Stern, the soaring **Siegessäule** (Victory Column) is an unabashed monument to Prussian militarism. It was completed in 1873, two years after the victory over the French, and also marks successes against Denmark (1864) and Austria (1866). A climb of around 285 steps takes you to the top of the 67m (220ft) column for a breathtaking view of the city from under the gilded bronze statue of Winged Victory.

During the 2006 World Cup, the Straße des 17. Juni, from here to the Brandenburg Gate, was the scene of the 'FIFA Fan Fest', probably the biggest soccer party in the world.

HAUS DER KULTUREN DER WELT

On the north side of the Großer Stern are monuments honouring the architects of that first unification, the Field Marshals Moltke and Roon, and Chancellor Bismarck. Follow the River Spree to the east along Spreeweg until you reach the former **Kongreßhalle**, built by the Americans as their contribution to the 1957 International Building Exhibition. Officially renamed **Haus der Kulturen der Welt** (House of World Cultures),

The Siegessäule

the striking design, with its curved concrete roof, led Berliners to dub the building the 'pregnant oyster'. In front of the building, the pond features a sculpture by Henry Moore, and is attractively illuminated at night. An austere black structure stands on the corner of Große Querallee near the Kongreßhalle. Built in 1987, the 42m- (138ft-) tall tower contains a 68-bell **carillon**, which chimes daily at noon and 6pm.

THE REICHSTAG

A few minutes' walk eastwards from the Haus der Kulturen der Welt, you will find the **Reichstag** ❺ building (S-Bahn Friedrichstraße; www.bundestag.de; daily 8am–11pm), its huge glass dome, with its mirrored central funnel, visible from much of the city and symbolic of a new Germany that keeps no secrets from its people. The parliamentary home of Wilhelminian and Weimar Germany displays the proud dedication *Dem deutschen Volke* (To the German People) on a neoclassical facade built in 1894 by Paul Wallot. This appeal to patriotism and democracy, set above six Corinthian columns, outlasted the burning in 1933 and the bombs of World War II, and was given renewed significance when Berlin resumed its former role as the seat of government of a unified Germany. Today, the dome, designed by Sir Norman Foster, is a major attraction for Berliners and tourists alike. They endure lengthy queues to be able to travel to the top, gazing out at the city and down into the Bundestag chamber. To join them, you must first register online.

The Reichstag now forms the centrepiece of what is otherwise a completely modern government quarter. Among the buildings spanning the bend in the River Spree stands the new **Federal Chancellery**, nicknamed the 'Washing Machine' by irreverent locals. Adjacent to the Reichstag, the river is straddled by an impressive complex designed by Stefan Braunfels: the **Paul-Löbe-Haus** on the south bank, housing the committee rooms of the Bundestag and parliamentarians' offices, linked by a bridge to the **Marie-Elisabeth-Lüders-Haus**, which houses archive and library facilities.

The largest modern complex in the Reichstag vicinity is the gigantic **Jakob-Kaiser-Haus**, behind the Reichstag itself, which is where the political parties have their headquarters and offices. Take a stroll past these offices and along the **promenade** that runs between the Reichstag and Friedrichstraße station. Among the features to look out for here are a sculpture representing the Berlin Wall – behind glass panelling with paragraphs of the German Constitution etched into it – and, near the Paul-Löbe-Haus, a metal memorial with white crosses on a black background, erected in honour of seven East Germans killed while attempting to flee to the West.

HAMBURGER BAHNHOF

Easily reached from the Reichstag via one of the Spree bridges, and within easy reach of the impressive Hauptbahnhof, are Invalidenstraße and two of Berlin's most fascinating museums. A splendid example of early railway architecture, the elegant old **Hamburger Bahnhof** (www.hamburgerbahnhof.de; Tue–Fri 10am–6pm, Thurs–8pm, Sat–Sun 11am–6pm; charge) is now the Museum of Contemporary Art, a spacious setting for works by modern masters like Joseph Beuys and Andy Warhol. Another venerable building, the 100-year-old **Museum für Naturkunde** ❻ (Natural History Museum; www.naturkundemuseum-berlin.de; Tue–Fri 9.30am–6pm, Sat–Sun 10am–6pm; charge) is one of the finest of its kind, with some 25 million objects in its collections. The famous dinosaur hall displays the world's largest dinosaur skeleton, a *Brachiosaurus*.

The promenade and memorial

BAUHAUS ARCHIV

Back in the Tiergarten, south of the Siegessäule at the corner of Stülerstraße and Klingelhöferstraße, stands the elegant, modern, shared complex that houses the **Embassies of the Nordic Countries** (Denmark, Finland, Norway, Sweden and Iceland). Completed in 1999, the architecture is a stunning showcase for Scandinavian design and materials.

Near the bridge over the Landwehrkanal, the stylised curves of the **Bauhaus Archiv** ❼ were designed by Walter Gropius, founder of the Bauhaus school of architecture, art and design. The **Museum für Gestaltung** (Design Museum; www.bauhaus.de; Wed–Mon 10am–5pm) documents the hugely influential achievements of the Bauhaus, the most progressive early 20th-century institution of its kind. Architects like Gropius himself, Mies van der Rohe and Marcel Breuer collaborated with artists such as Paul Klee, Vasili Kandinsky, Lyonel Feininger, Oskar Schlemmer and Laszlo Moholy-Nagy, in an attempt to integrate arts, crafts and architecture into mass industrial society. On view here is a selection of the objects they created; tubular steel chairs, cups and saucers, teapots, desks, new weaves for carpets, chess pieces and children's building blocks, as well as some pioneering architectural plans and sketches.

STAUFFENBERGSTRASSE

Follow the north bank of the tree-lined Landwehrkanal along the Reichpietschufer as far as Stauffenbergstraße. On the corner stands one of Berlin's most striking works of Modernist architecture, the **Gasag Building** (or Shell Haus), designed by Emil Fahrenkamp and built for Shell Oil in 1930. This was one of the first steel-framed 'high-rise' buildings in Berlin. Its flowing curves, lightness of style and use of glass provide a stark contrast to the Nazi architecture built later in the 1930s, as seen, for example, in the Japanese Embassy on nearby Hildebrandstraße, or indeed at the next attraction. The **Gedenkstätte Deutscher Widerstand** (www.gdw-berlin. de; Mon–Fri 9am–6pm, Thur 9am–8pm, Sat–Sun 10am–6pm) at Stauffenbergstraße 13–14 is a memorial to German resistance against the Nazi regime, located within the *Bendlerblock*, the former German military headquarters. A bronze statue depicting a young man with bound hands stands in the courtyard where Graf von Stauffenberg and other army officers who conspired to blow up Hitler on 20 July 1944, were shot. An excellent exhibition, in the rooms of the building where the attempted coup was planned, charts the tragic course of resistance.

Follow Stauffenbergstraße to its junction with Tiergartenstraße. At the corner is the **Austrian Embassy**. Designed by Austrian architect Hans Hollein and completed in 2001,

The Bauhaus Archiv building

its three distinct parts rendered in turquoise, lilac and grey, reflect the different functions within the building. The embassy marks the eastern gateway to the diplomatic quarter, which runs along Tiergartenstraße to the left. In the other direction, Tiergartenstraße leads straight to the Kulturforum.

KULTURFORUM

Situated just west of Potsdamer Platz, the **Kulturforum** (S-Bahn/U-Bahn Potsdamer Platz) is a complex of concert halls and museums built on land levelled by the plans of Albert Speer, Hitler's architect, to redesign the city and then the bombs of World War II. It is clustered around the only building to survive from previous eras, the **Matthäikirche**, which was built in the neo-Romanesque style in 1846 by August Stüler and stands in dignified isolation on Matthäikirchplatz.

The Merchant Georg Gisze by Hans Holbein the Younger

The quality of exhibits in the museums here is outstanding. Completed in 1998, the **Gemäldegalerie 8** (www.smb.museum; Tue–Sun 10am–6pm, Thur until 8pm; charge) is home to a remarkable collection of German and European paintings from the 13th to the 19th centuries. Among the works are masterpieces such as Hans Holbein's

Portrait of the Merchant Georg Gisze (1532); the rather amusing *The Fountain of Youth* (1546) by Lucas Cranach the Elder; Van Eyck's *Portrait of Giovanni Arnolfini* (1440); Van Dyck's portraits of a Genoese couple (1626); Vermeer's study, *Young Lady with a Pearl Necklace* (1644); and, among one of the largest Rembrandt collections in the world, a portrait of the artist's second wife, Hendrickje Stoffels (1659).

Adjacent to the gallery, the **Kunstgewerbemuseum** (www.smb.museum) displays a wide range of the most exquisitely executed arts and crafts, from medieval times to the present day. Among its outstanding treasures is the Welfenschatz, comprising dazzling examples of the goldsmith's art from the 11th to the 15th centuries – richly bejewelled crosses, reliquaries and portable altars, presented to St Blasius Cathedral in Brunswick by successive generations of Guelph (Welf) dukes. Other prized exhibits include glazed Italian majolica and a quite bewitching collection of porcelain – Chinese, Meissen, Frankenthal, Nymphenburg, as well as Berlin's own Königliche Porzellan Manufaktur (the royal KPM). The museum is undergoing much-needed restoration and is closed to the public.

The **Kupferstichkabinett** (Prints and Drawings Collection; www.smb.museum; Tue–Fri 10am–6pm, Sat–Sun 11am–6pm; charge) is one of the world's finest graphics collections, with works ranging from 14th-century illuminated manuscripts to modern woodcuts by Erich Heckel and lithographs by Willem de Kooning. Also on display are outstanding works by Dürer, Botticelli and Rembrandt.

The architect Hans Scharoun is famous for his Expressionistic free-form structures. His first design, the controversial ochre and gold **Philharmonie ⑨** (www.berliner-philharmoniker.de), owes its tent-like shape to the demands of the concert hall's acoustics and sight-lines. The home of the Berlin Philharmonic Orchestra was designed from the inside out, from the orchestra to the walls and roof. Viewed from across Tiergartenstraße, the nearby **Musik-instrumentenmuseum** (www.sim.spk-berlin.de; Tue–Fri 9am–5pm, Thur–10pm, Sat–Sun 10am–5pm; charge), also by Scharoun, is reminiscent of an open card index file. Its extensive collection of instruments from the 16th century to the present day includes a 1703 Stradivarius violin, the 1810 piano of composer Carl Maria von Weber, and a 1929 New York Wurlitzer cinema organ, which comes alive in a concert given at noon every Saturday. Tours are conducted every Saturday at 11am and Thursday at 6pm.

Scharoun also designed the nearby **Staatsbibliothek** (State Library; Potsdamer Straße 33; http://staatsbibliothek-berlin.de). Despite its formidable dimensions, the library is a model of peace and harmony. A quite ingenious network of staircases leads to multi-level reading rooms and easily accessible stacks. This is one of the largest modern library buildings in

The Neue Nationalgalerie with Henry Moore's bronze 'Archer'

Europe, and it regularly holds exhibitions and concerts.

NEUE NATIONALGALERIE

Just south of the Matthäi-kirche at the corner of Pots-damer Straße, though not part of the Kulturforum, is

Early birds

With popular temporary exhibitions, the queue for the Neue Nationalgalerie often stretches right round the building; try to get there early.

the **Neue Nationalgalerie** ❿ (www.smb.museum; Tue–Fri 10am–6pm, Thur–8pm, Sat–Sun 11am–6pm; charge; closed for renovation until 2019). This square, glass-wall structure with its vast, black steel roof supported by eight massive steel columns, was designed by Bauhaus master Mies van der Rohe and completed in 1968, a year before his death. The building is of characteristic elegant simplicity and consid-ered a prime example of structural abstraction emblematic of the International Style. It stands on a raised granite plat-form that serves as a sculpture court for huge pieces like Henry Moore's *Archer*.

The gallery houses an outstanding collection of 20th-century painting and sculpture, the main focus being on Cubism, Expressionism, Bauhaus and Surrealism. The works of Picasso, Gris, Leger and Lauens show the development of Cubism, while Expressionism is represented by some nota-ble works of Max Beckmann, as well as artists from the *Die Brücke* group, with works by Kirchner (*Potsdamer Platz*, 1914), Schmidt-Rottluff and Heckel. Surrealist paintings by Max Ernst, Salvador Dalí and Joán Miró are also displayed, as are New Objectivity works by Otto Dix and George Grosz. Exponents of the Bauhaus style represented here include Kandinsky and Klee; there are also some American paintings from the 1960s and 1970s, including abstract works by Frank Stella and Ellsworth Kelly. During temporary exhibitions held over long

A piece of the past

A poignant contrast to the futuristic architecture and technological content of the Sony Center can be found in the elegant remains of the old Grandhotel Esplanade, now preserved behind glass walls at the entrance. Before it was almost completely destroyed during World War II, the hotel was a meeting point for the international rich and famous, including stars such as Greta Garbo and Charlie Chaplin.

periods several times a year, the gallery's permanent collection is not on view.

POTSDAMER PLATZ

Reduced by war and the Wall to a bleak no-man's-land, **Potsdamer Platz** ⑪, the square that was at one time the busiest in Europe, has burst back into life in the most bracing fashion. What was once a scar on the landscape, epitomising the division of the city and country, is now a thriving arts, entertainment, shopping and business centre. The impact of the towering, modern buildings, made predominantly from glass, is astounding. Investment from corporations such as Daimler-Chrysler and Sony has resulted in the construction of shopping malls, a theatre, a casino, some great hotels, cinemas and a film museum.

Almost 100,000 people arrive here daily to marvel at the striking architecture and explore the latest attractions in this city-within-a-city. The **Sony Center** is an entertainment complex, contained within a central courtyard under a glass ceiling. Technophiles can check out the latest gadgets at Sony's first European department store, while film fans can visit the **Film Museum Berlin** (www.deutsche-kinemathek.de; Tue–Sun 10am–6pm, Thur until 8pm; charge). This absorbing museum commemorates the city's history in cinema production, and pays tribute to the greatest of German screen stars, Marlene Dietrich. Also here is the **Television Museum** covering landmarks in German broadcasting.

The Kohlhoff Tower opposite the Sony Center is worth a visit for its **Panoramapunkt** viewing platform (Potsdamer Platz 1; www.panoramapunkt.de; daily 10am–8pm; charge), offering a grand view of central Berlin.

Situated to the immediate north of the Sony Center, the 18-storey **Beisheim Center**, housing the Ritz Carlton Hotel, and 17-storey **Delbrück-Haus**, provide a skyline reminiscent of Art Deco skyscrapers in New York and Chicago.

Stretching away to the south of the Sony Center, the Arkaden shopping centre became a firm favourite with city shoppers as soon as it opened in 1998, and the cafés, casino and theatres in Marlene-Dietrich-Platz are equally popular.

A touch of New York or Chicago at Potsdamer Platz

SOUTH OF POTSDAMER PLATZ

The **Martin-Gropius-Bau**, situated nearby at Stresemann Straße 110, was originally built as an arts and crafts museum. Erected between 1877 and 1881 by Martin Gropius (great-uncle of the Bauhaus's Walter Gropius), with the help of Heino Schmieden, the lavish red and gold building is now a spacious exhibition centre.

Art and architecture exhibits are displayed in and around its skylighted inner courtyard area.

Adjacent to the Martin-Gropius-Bau is the site of Prinz-Albrecht-Straße 8, the former School of Applied Arts and Design, which served as the headquarters of the SS, Gestapo and other Nazi institutions. Excavations in 1987 revealed cellars where thousands of victims were imprisoned and tortured.

The building constructed above the former Gestapo and SS headquarters houses the **Topographie des Terrors** ⓬, an outdoor and indoor museum that illustrates the persecution of those who resisted the Nazi terror. Berlin has many reminders of its dark past, but this place has particular impact. A section of the Berlin Wall remains in place next to the site.

Further along at Askanischer Platz is the restored ruin of the entrance portico of **Anhalter Bahnhof**. The old railway station was the work of Franz Schwechten, the architect who designed that other noble ruin, the Kaiser Wilhelm Memorial Church (see page 34).

ANHALTER BAHNHOF

Anhalter Bahnhof was once Berlin's most glamorous railway station, linking the city to Europe's other great capitals. Its west-bound platform staged the tragic last act of the Weimar Republic: soon after Hitler became Chancellor, Berlin's most gifted artists and intellectuals – among them Heinrich Mann, Bertolt Brecht, Kurt Weill, Georg Grosz and Albert Einstein – gathered here, their bags packed for the 'last train to freedom'. The station was patched up after the war, but after the border was sealed it stood at the end of a line to nowhere, and became redundant. Today, all that remains of Anhalter Bahnhof is the restored entrance portico to the main hall; the land on which the station itself once stood is covered by playing fields and Berlin's tent-like Tempodrom events venue.

You can't miss the **Deutsches Technikmuseum Berlin** ⓭ (U-Bahn Gleisdreieck, S-Bahn Anhalter Bahnhof; www.sdtb.de; Tue–Fri 9am–5.30pm, Sat–Sun 10am–6pm; charge) on the banks of the Landwehrkanal: poised over its entrance is the front end of one of the original transport planes from the Berlin Airlift, a Douglas DC3. Built over the freight yards of the Anhalter Bahnhof, this is one of the city's most fascinating museums, with exhibits dealing with all aspects of transport and technology, from railways, aviation, shipping and road transport to textiles, medicine, communications and printing. In the Spectrum section you can use various bits of machinery and participate in experiments.

Deutsches Technikmuseum, complete with DC3

ON AND AROUND UNTER DEN LINDEN

The area east of the Brandenburg Gate, known as Mitte (Middle), is the historic centre of Berlin, and was once the centre of the capital of the German Democratic Republic (GDR). The city's most important museums, government buildings churches and theatres were constructed here in the 18th–20th centuries. Many buildings were restored by the GDR after Allied bombing in World War II, and several quarters were almost completely rebuilt in their old style, notably Gendarmenmarkt

Brandenburg Gate

and Museumsinsel (see pages 57 and 61). Since reunification, restoration continued apace, facades returned to their former glory and some striking new additions were made by internationally acclaimed architects. Today, the area's principal avenue, **Unter den Linden**, has regained its former importance as the main focus of the capital's cultural and political life, while nearby Friedrichstraße is once again Berlin's fashionable shopping artery.

BRANDENBURG GATE

Once the scene of great military parades and processions, this formidable symbol of the united city appears at last to be realising the vision of Johann Gottfried Schadow, the sculptor who crowned the **Brandenburger Tor** ⓮ with the Quadriga, a copper statue of Winged Victory in her four-horse chariot. Schadow had wanted the gate to be known as the *Friedenstor* (Gate of Peace), in keeping with the relief of the *Procession of*

Peace that he himself had sculpted beneath Victory's simple chariot.

The gate itself, designed by Carl Gotthard Langhans, was built between 1789 and 1791. With two rows of six Doric columns forming the gateway proper, it was inspired by the Propylaeum gatehouse leading to the Parthenon in Athens. Forming part of the city wall, the gate was intended by the pragmatic Prussians not so much as a triumphal arch as an imposing tollgate for collecting duties.

The gate was left isolated in no-man's land when the Wall went up, and subsequently became the scene of quite ecstatic celebrations when the Wall came down, though this may now seem difficult to believe as Berliners walk nonchalantly from east to west through the Brandenburg Gate's mighty central arch. The north wing of the Gate houses a 'quiet room' where visitors can sit and contemplate in peace; the south wing houses a **BERLIN infostore**.

PARISER PLATZ

In front of the Brandenburg Gate is the cobbled Pariser Platz, an expansive square surrounded by buildings of varying styles, including the **French Embassy** on the left. On the right looking east, the square is dominated by the smartest hotel in town, the supremely elegant **Hotel Adlon Kempinski**, rebuilt on the site of the original Hotel Adlon, a 1920s Berlin legend. On the square at the side of the Adlon is the glass facade of the **Akademie der Künste** designed by Günter Behnisch. Next to that, the **DZ Bank** building designed by Californian architect Frank Gehry gives little clue as to what lies inside – a remarkable atrium covered by a vaulted glass roof said to have the form of a fish, beneath which a walk-in sculpture resembling Captain Nemo's *Nautilus* is in fact the outer skin of a conference room. Visitors can go in, but no further than the entrance

The British Embassy

hall's security turnstiles. Security measures of an entirely different order have also been deployed around the adjacent **US Embassy**.

HOLOCAUST MEMORIAL

A passage through the Akademie der Künste leads to the **Holocaust Mahnmal** (memorial, www.holocaust-mahnmal.de), which runs south along Friedrich-Ebert-Straße in the direction of Potsdamer Platz. New York architect Peter Eisenman's concept is deliberately disorientating; an extensive area of ground planted with 2,700 concrete pillars of differing heights and no designated entrance or exit. There is an information centre underneath.

UNTER DEN LINDEN TO FRIEDRICHSTRASSE

Sweeping eastwards from Pariser Platz, the grand 61m (200ft) -wide avenue, literally named 'Beneath the Linden Trees', was Berlin's showcase boulevard. Frederick the Great saw it as the centre of his royal capital, and it became the most prestigious address in town. Some of its splendour fell victim to 19th-century building speculation, but the avenue remained fashionable until the bombs of World War II reduced it to rubble. Now the trees have been replanted and most of the important buildings have been restored.

A short distance down on the right is Wilhelmstraße (blocked to traffic by concrete blocks because of security fears). Until World War II this was where the British Embassy was situated, as was the Reichspräsidentenpalais (Palace of the President of the Reich), the Foreign Office, the Reichskanzlei (Chancellery) as well as many other ministries. The **British Embassy** is now in a striking building (No 70/71) designed by Michael Wilford and Partners.

A little further down on the right is the **Embassy of the Russian Federation**. If you take a right then a left onto Behrenstraße, you will see the unprepossessing modern facade of the **Komische Oper**, one of Berlin's three opera companies. The ugly exterior is the result of post-war reconstruction; happily, the magnificently over-the-top gilded interior has been retained.

Across Unter den Linden from the Russian Embassy is Berlin's branch of **Madame Tussauds** (www.madametussauds. com; daily 10am–7pm, Aug until 9pm; charge), where you can rub shoulders with the likes of Bismarck, Boris Becker, Karl Marx and Angela Merkel.

FRIEDRICHSTRASSE

About half way along, Friedrichstraße crosses Unter den Linden. Much new building work was completed along this famous street in the early part of the noughties, both to the north where Friedrichstraße has been restored and to the south where architectural monstrosities built during the days of the GDR have been demolished and replaced by

Holocaust Memorial

Jewish Museum interior

a very elegant development of designer shops, offices and apartments. French élan came to Berlin in the form of a branch of the famous department store, **Galeries Lafayette**, at Quartier 207. The sophisticated art deco styling of Quartier 206 is home to some very exclusive designer boutiques.

Towards the southern end of Friedrichstraße, huge suspended pictures of a Soviet and a US soldier mark the site of **Checkpoint Charlie**, that infamous border crossing between East and West. Six weeks after the building of the Wall, it was here that American and Russian tanks faced each other in what was one of the tensest stand-offs of the Cold War. Today, the barbed wire and barriers are gone, but the memories remain. Right on the spot is an open-air exhibition about the major historic events that took place here. Next to it, the **Haus am Checkpoint Charlie** ⓯ (U-Bahn Kochstraße; www.mauermuseum.de; daily 9am–10pm; charge) celebrates the ingenuity and courage of those who sought to escape to the West, and commemorates those who died doing so.

JEWISH MUSEUM

Memories of human tragedy on an even wider scale can be found at the **Jüdisches Museum** ⓰ (U-Bahn Hallesches Tor; www.jmberlin.de; Mon 10am–10pm, Tue–Sun 10am–8pm; charge), further south on Lindenstraße. With its jagged outline and its disorientating interior of sloping galleries and unexpected angles, Daniel Libeskind's striking zinc-faced building symbolises the troubled course of Jewish life in Germany and the devastation of the Holocaust. Its exhibits give a comprehensive and moving account.

GENDARMENMARKT

From Friedrichstraße, follow Jägerstraße or Taubenstraße to reach **Gendarmenmarkt** ⑰, the celebrated architectural ensemble south of Unter den Linden. This grand square, bordered by bookshops and cafés set in delightful arcades, has been almost completely restored after being blasted to smithereens during World War II. The imposing **Schiller-Denkmal** (1868), a monument sculpted in Carrara marble, surrounds a statue of the writer Friedrich von Schiller with the muses of philosophy, poetry, drama and history. It stands in front of Schinkel's Ionic-porticoed **Konzerthaus**. Originally called the Schauspielhaus (Playhouse), this is now a concert hall. It stands between two identical churches, the **Französischer Dom** (or French Cathedral) to the north, built for the immigrant Huguenots, and the **Deutscher Dom** (German Cathedral) to the south. Both were built in the early 18th century. The domes were added in 1785.

Deutscher Dom

Scholarly greats

Among the renowned academics to work at the Humboldt University were the philosophers Hegel and Schleiermacher, philologists Jacob and Wilhelm Grimm, physicists Max Planck, Albert Einstein and Otto Hahn and physicians Virchow, Koch and Sauerbruch.

Step inside the Französischer Dom to visit the **Hugenottenmuseum**, or look up the stairwell to the Glockenspiel – a dizzying 48m (159ft) above. The Deutscher Dom houses an excellent exhibition about Germany's recent social and political history, cleverly combining documents, photographs and radio broadcasts to chronicle the rise of Nazism and the development of democracy. Audio guides are available in English.

UNTER DEN LINDEN TO SCHLOSSBRÜCKE

East of Charlottenstraße is the patched, dark stone of the **Deutsche Staatsbibliothek** (German State Library), the former Prussian State Library, built between 1903 and 1914 but damaged during World War II. Adjacent is the **Humboldt Universität**. The main building was erected between 1748–66 by Johann Boumann as a palace for Prince Heinrich, the brother of Frederick II. In 1810, on the initiative of the eminent scientists Alexander and Wilhelm von Humboldt, it was converted to a seat of learning. At this point an imposing **statue of Frederick the Great on Horseback** (1851), by Christian Daniel Rauch, stands in the avenue's central strip.

Heinrich's Palace was just part of a grand scheme commissioned by Frederick the Great to recreate the cultural climate that his grandfather had brought to Berlin during the 17th century. Known as the Forum Fridericianum, the major portion of the scheme occupies the other side of Unter den Linden around the open square called **Bebelplatz** (formerly Opernplatz), which was the scene of book-burning by Nazi students in 1933. On the west side is the curving Baroque facade of the **Alte Bibliothek** (Old Library). Facing it to the east is the grand Palladian-style **Staatsoper Unter den Linden** (State Opera) designed in 1742 by von Knobelsdorff, Frederick the Great's favourite architect. To the south of the Staatsoper on the corner of Bebelplatz is **St Hedwigs-Kathedrale**, from 1747, a huge, domed structure built for the Catholics incorporated into Protestant Prussia by Frederick's conquest of Silesia. To the east of the square, the **Operncafé** is housed in the Prinzessinnenpalais, the Prussian princesses' Baroque town house. Its open-air terrace is one of the most popular places to meet on Unter den Linden, while inside there is an elegant café and a restaurant.

Beside the university, the **Neue Wache** ⓲ (New Guardhouse; daily 10am–6pm; free) was Karl Friedrich Schinkel's

The Neue Wache, built by Karl Friedrich Schinkel

first important building, completed in 1818. After serving as the GDR's 'Memorial to the Victims of Fascism and Militarism', the little neoclassical structure now commemorates all victims of war and tyranny. Inside is Käthe Kollwitz's poignant sculpture *Grieving Mother*.

Next door is the handsome, Baroque **Zeughaus**, once arsenal for the Prussian Army, as the sculpted suits of armour testify along the roof. The artist Andreas Schlüter (see box below) provided the military sculpture, but was able to assert more pacifistic views with poignant sculpted masks of dying warriors (1696) in the inner courtyard named after him, the **Schlüterhof**.

Now splendidly restored and with a glittering annexe by the American architect I.M. Pei, the Zeughaus is the home of the **Deutsches Historisches Museum** (www.dhm.de; daily 10am–6pm; charge), with rich collections on national history.

ARCHITECTS OF BERLIN

An outstanding sculptor and architect, Andreas Schlüter (1664–1714) gave the city much of its Baroque appearance. Look for the 21 masks of dying soldiers in the Zeughaus courtyard (Schlüterhof) in Unter den Linden, and the equestrian statue of Friedrich Wilhelm, 'Der Große Kurfürst' (the Great Elector), outside Schloss Charlottenburg.

Georg Wenzeslaus von Knobelsdorff (1699–1753) was Frederick the Great's favourite architect. Among his greatest achievements are St Hedwigs-Kathedrale, the Staatsoper Unter den Linden, the new wing at Schloss Charlottenburg, and Schloss Sanssouci in Potsdam.

Karl Friedrich Schinkel (1781–1841) was Berlin's most gifted and prolific neoclassical architect. His other talents were landscape painting and stage design. Works include the Neue Wache and the Altes Museum, the Schauspielhaus at Gendarmenmarkt, and the neo-Gothic war memorial in Viktoria Park, Kreuzberg.

Linking Unter den Linden to Karl-Liebknecht-Straße is the exquisite **Schlossbrücke**  (Palace Bridge), designed by Schinkel in 1820–24, but built after his death in the 1850s, and adorned with fierce warriors and victory goddesses.

MUSEUM ISLAND

Beyond the bridge, the imposing neoclassical facade of the Altes Museum at the far end of the Lustgarten (Pleasure Garden), forms a grand entrance to **Museumsinsel** (U-Bahn/

Statue on the Schlossbrücke

S-Bahn Friedrichstraße, S-Bahn Hackescher Markt), the site of Berlin's most important museums.

The **Altes Museum** (www.smb.museum; Tue–Sun 10am–6pm, Thur 10am–8pm; charge) is a fine neoclassical building, generally regarded as Schinkel's masterpiece. The massive polished granite bowl in front was originally intended to sit atop the edifice. The museum houses an astonishing collection of Greek and Roman antiquities.

Beyond Bodestraße is the **Alte Nationalgalerie** ❷⓿ (www. smb.museum; Tue–Sun 10am–6pm, Thur 10am–8pm; charge), a temple to 19th-century art. Among the most interesting works are the lively canvases of Carl Blechen. There are also works by Max Liebermann (*The Flax Workers* and portraits of Wilhelm von Bode and Richard Strauss), and by Adolph von Menzel, whose *Eisenwalzwerk* (The Iron Foundry, 1875) is a striking portrayal of industrial labour. Rooms on the upper floor house a fine collection of works by early 19th-century Romantic painters; the 24 paintings by Caspar David Friedrich here constitute the largest number of works by him under one roof. Among them, look for *Abtei im Eichwald* (Abbey in the Oakwood, 1809) and *Der Mönch am Meer* (The Monk by the Sea, 1810). The Friedrich collection is complemented by 15 of Karl Friedrich Schinkel's paintings of imaginative landscapes and architectural visions.

Further north is the **Pergamonmuseum** ㉑ (Am Kupfergraben; www.smb.museum; daily 10am–6pm, Thur until 8pm; charge, parts closed for renovation until 2019), home to many impressive works of classical antiquity, the Near East, Islam and the Orient. The museum is named after its most prized

Pergamon Altar detail

possession: the gigantic **Pergamon Altar** (2nd century BC). This Hellenistic masterpiece came from what is now Bergama, on Turkey's west coast. Dedicated to Zeus and Athena, it occupies an entire hall of the museum.

The **Babylonian Processional Street** (604–562BC), built by King Nebuchadnezzar II, is equally impressive. Lions sculpted in relief stride along the street's blue-and-ochre tiled walls towards the Ishtar Gate. The gate itself is decorated with bulls and dragons, also in blue-and-ochre tiles.

A third great treasure is the Roman **Market Gate of Miletus**, from Greek Asia Minor (AD165). Its name belies the true character of this elaborate monument, which constitutes both gateway and shopping complex.

The **Islamic Museum** in the Pergamon's south wing exhibits the grand facade of the 8th-century **Palace of Mshatta** (from what is now Jordan). It is embellished with intricately incised or perforated animal and plant motifs. Among the other exhibits are some exquisite Indian **Mogul miniatures**.

The head of Queen Nefertiti

Next to the Pergamonmuseum is the **Neues Museum** ㉒ (www.neues-museum.de; daily 10am–6pm, Thur until 8pm; charge). Erected between 1843 and 1855 according to plans by Friedrich August Stüler, it was badly bombed in World War II and restored by architect David Chipperfield. It houses the Museum of Prehistory and Early History as well as the **Egyptian Museum**, which covers 3,000 years of sculpture, papyrus fragments and hieroglyphic tablets. The most famous piece in the collection is the beautiful head of **Queen Nefertiti** (1340BC), consort of Akhenaton. The bust had been buried for over 3,000 years, before German and French archaeologists unearthed it in 1912. Other highlights of the collection include: the Berlin Green Head with its wrinkled features, mummies and sarcophagi, and blue faience funerary objects in the shape of animals.

The final great institution of Museumsinsel, at the very tip of the island, is the **Bodemuseum** (Monbijou-brücke; www.smb. museum; Tue–Sun 10am–6pm, Thur until 8pm; charge). It houses Early Christian and Byzantine Art, ancient coins, sculpture, and paintings from the Middle Ages to the 18th century.

BERLIN CATHEDRAL & AROUND

On the north side of the Lustgarten stands Kaiser Wilhelm II's **Berliner Dom** ㉓. The imposing exterior has been completely restored, and its interior beautifully renovated, despite heavy bomb damage in World War II. The cathedral's crypt contains 95 Hohenzollern sarcophagi.

On the other side of the Spree, across **Friedrichbrücke**, is the superb **DDR Museum** (www.ddr-museum.de; daily 10am–8pm, Sat–10pm; charge). It provides an intriguing and honest insight into everyday life in the old East Germany, including a mock-up DDR apartment, a Trabant car and a Stasi interrogation room.

The Red Town Hall and Television Tower

AROUND ALEXANDERPLATZ

On the opposite side of the Lustgarten stands the area once more known as **Schlossplatz**. Under the GDR its name was changed to Marx-Engels-Platz, and it became a focus of Communist May Day military parades and rallies. The war-damaged Stadtschloss (City Palace) of the Hohenzollerns once stood here. However, in 1950 Walter Ulbricht decided to raze it as a symbol of German imperialism, despite protests from art historians that it was the city's outstanding Baroque building. The palace balcony where Spartacist leader Karl Liebknecht proclaimed his doomed 'Socialist Republic' in 1918 was added to the front of the former **Staatsrat** (Council of State) on the east side of the square, while the bronze, glass and steel Palast der Republik – once East Germany's parliament – replaced what remained of the royal residence. In 2009, the decaying Palast had its date with the wrecking ball clearing space for the reconstruction of the original palace, which will house the Humboldt Forum (http://sbs-humboldtforum.de), an international exhibition of art, culture and science.

Continue along Karl-Liebknecht-Straße as far as the **Marienkirche** (13th century) on former Neuer Markt, a haven of sober Gothic simplicity amid the prevailing bombast. Inside, see Andreas Schlüter's Baroque marble pulpit (1703) and a late-Gothic fresco of the *Dance of Death* (1484).

The neo-Renaissance Berliner Rathaus, also known as the **Rotes Rathaus ㉔** (Red Town Hall), owes its nickname to its red clinker masonry, not its ideology. Built between 1861 and 1869, it is now the seat of the city's governing mayor, and is decorated with a terracotta frieze chronicling the history of Berlin.

ALEXANDERPLATZ

Beyond the huge **Neptunbrunnen** (Neptune's Fountain) of 1891, an elaborate affair decorated with four figures representing the rivers Rhine, Elbe, Oder and Vistula, you can't miss the **Fernsehturm ㉕** (Television Tower) rising up above Alexanderplatz. It was built in 1969, and at 368m (1,207ft) dwarfs western Berlin's Funkturm (see page 74), which was the object of the exercise. Not for the fainthearted, an observation deck at 207m (679ft) affords fine views over the city, while the revolving restaurant provides refreshment.

'Alex', as the huge square is known, was the heart of pre-war Berlin, and its vibrancy was celebrated in Alfred Döblin's great 1929 novel Berlin Alexanderplatz, later filmed by Rainer Werner Fassbinder. Renovation work during the Noughties saw the addition of several major buildings, including shopping malls and Berlin's largest underground railway station, with plans mooted for further buildings.

NIKOLAIVIERTEL

South of the Rotes Rathaus, the Nikolai neighbourhood was restored for Berlin's 750th anniversary celebrations in 1987. The site of Berlin's earliest settlement, the whole district is now a kind of open-air museum. Its focal point is Berlin's oldest church, the twin-steepled Romanesque and Gothic **Nikolaikirche**, begun in 1230. Among the buildings resurrected here is the **Gaststätte zum Nußbaum**, the favourite tavern of cartoonist Heinrich Zille. Some of his works can be seen in the **Heinrich Zille Museum Berlin** nearby (Propststraße 11; www.heinrich-zille-museum.de; daily 11am–6pm Nov–Mar, until 7pm Apr–Oct; charge). The **Knoblauchhaus**, at Poststraße 23, is an elegant house rebuilt in neoclassical style in 1835 and containing some fine Biedermeier furniture. Statelier is the reconstructed Ephraimpalais (Poststraße 16), a rococo mansion built for Friedrich II's financier Veitel Heine Ephraim in 1765. Today the **Museum Ephraim-Palais** (www.stadtmuseum.de; Tue and Thur–Sun 10am–6pm, Wed noon–8pm; charge) presents three floors of exhibitions on the history of Berlin's arts and culture.

MÄRKISCHES MUSEUM

On the other side of the Spree, across the Jannowitzbrücke, stands the red-brick **Märkisches Museum** (U-Bahn

Märkisches Museum; www.stadtmuseum.de; Tue–Sun 10am–6pm; charge). With a wealth of exhibits, the museum tells the story of Berlin from the Middle Ages to the present. Odd bits of Berliniana include early sewing machines, bicycles, telephones, and an 1881 phone book with just 41 names. The building itself is worthy of attention – its Gothic chapel, guildhall and arms hall have all been restored to their original state.

ORANIENBURGER STRASSE

On the north side of the River Spree, **Oranienburger Straße** is the heart of the old Jewish quarter. In the 1920s, a diverse community of Jewish professionals and bohemian artists and writers lived, worked and thrived here. The area has now regained much of its former vibrancy

Picturesque street in Nikolaiviertel

after the devastation of the war and the grim sterility of its aftermath. Cultural centres and Jewish restaurants rub shoulders with off-beat cafés and alternative art venues beneath the magnificent black-and-gold-leafed dome of the **Neue Synagoge** (www.centrumjudaicum.de). The biggest synagogue in Germany, designed by Eduard Knoblauch and completed in 1866, it was saved during the anti-Semitic attacks of Kristallnacht on 9 November 1938, but later destroyed by Allied bombing. Its facade was beautifully restored and exhibits from the adjacent centre of Jewish studies, Centrum Judaicum, are displayed here.

Nearby **Hackesche Höfe** ㉖ is a fascinating complex of early 20th-century courtyards. Beautifully restored, this is now a lively spot, with bars, art galleries, shops, offices, and even a theatre. The adjacent **Anne Frank Zentrum** features an exhibition devoted to the life of Anne Frank (Rosenthaler Straße 39, S-Bahn Hackescher Markt; www.annefrank.de; Tue–Sun 10am–6pm; charge).

Walk the Wall

Traces of the Wall in today's Berlin can prove hard to track down. A GPS WallGuide can be rented from the East Side Gallery, the Checkpoint Charlie Museum and other Wall-related locations. It directs you to key sites and points of interest along the former Wall, giving detailed audio and video information in English. For rental points and to watch a sample, go to www.mauerguide.com.

KARL-MARX-ALLEE

Known until 1961 as Stalin-Allee, **Karl-Marx-Allee** ㉗ runs southeast from Alexanderplatz. It is worth coming here to look at the facades of the **Stalinesque-style apartment blocks** that line the avenue on both sides, and which, as far as Frankfurter Tor, have been superbly restored. Whether or not you are a fan of the style, you cannot fail to be impressed by the sheer scale of the enterprise.

South of Karl-Marx-Allee along Mühlenstraße, between Ostbahnhof and Oberbaum-brücke, a section of the Berlin Wall has been preserved as the **East Side Gallery** (www. eastsidegallery-berlin.de). A variety of international artists painted murals here in 1990, after the collapse of the Wall, and many of them have since been restored. You can still see some of the iconic images of that era, including *Brotherly Kiss* by Dimitri Vrubel, which depicts a smooching Leonid Brezhnev and Erich Honecker.

The Neue Synagoge

PRENZLAUER BERG

To the north of Alexanderplatz, Schönhauser Allee leads to the centre of **Prenzlauer Berg**, a 19th-century working-class quar-ter; now a lively, bohemian area with colourful nightlife, plenty of cafés and restaurants, and entertainment complexes such as the **Kulturbrauerei** ㉘, a converted brewery. The artist Käthe Kollwitz (see page 33) lived here. A colourful market is held around the central Kollwitzplatz every Thursday and Saturday.

OUTSIDE THE CENTRE
SCHLOSS CHARLOTTENBURG

An exemplary piece of Prussian Baroque and rococo architec-ture and decoration, **Schloss Charlottenburg** ㉙ is the city's only

Fine furnishings

To try to recapture the interior's rather gracious rococo atmosphere, furniture and decorations from other 18th-century Prussian palaces have been used to replace what was destroyed at Charlottenburg during World War II.

surviving major Hohenzollern residence. Badly damaged in a World War II air raid, it became the target of extensive post-war reconstruction, and is now the focal point of a number of the city's most fascinating museums. To do the palace, grounds and surrounding museums full justice, you will need to spend at least a day here.

Schloss Charlottenburg (www.spsg.de; Apr–Oct Tue–Sun 10am–6pm, Nov–Mar until 5pm; charge) was conceived as a summer retreat for the future Queen Sophie Charlotte in the 1690s, when the site beside the River Spree, west of the Tiergarten, lay well outside the city limits. It was a small palace – scarcely one-fifth of the huge structure you see today – and only with the addition of a majestic domed tower (with the goddess Fortune as its weathervane), the Orangerie to the west and a new east wing, did it become big enough for Frederick the Great. If he ever had to leave his beloved Potsdam, this was where he came.

In the palace courtyard you will find an **equestrian statue** of the Great Elector Friedrich Wilhelm, designed by Schlüter in 1697. One of many art works lost in World War II, it was finally recovered from Tegel Lake in 1949, where it had sunk with the barge that was taking it to safety.

In the **Gobelinzimmer**, notice the fine 18th-century tapestries by Charles Vigne. The rays of light on the ceiling of the **Audienzzimmer** (Reception Room) and bright yellow damask walls in the **Schlafzimmer** (bedroom) imitate the motif of the Sun King, Louis XIV, the Prussian rulers' hero. Chinoiserie is the dominating feature of the opulent **Porzellankabinett**, filled with hundreds of pieces of Chinese and Japanese porcelain. The relatively sober **Japanische Kammer** contains prized lacquered cabinets and tables, and tapestries that depict landscapes in China. The **Eichengalerie** (Oak Gallery) is filled with portraits of the Hohenzollern family. Chamber music recitals can be heard in the **Eosander-Kapelle** (chapel), which has extravagant rococo decor.

Designed for Frederick the Great by Georg von Knobelsdorff, the **Neuer Flügel** (new wing, also the east wing – under renovation) subtly combines dignified late-Baroque facades with exuberant rococo interiors. The ceremonial staircase that leads to Frederick the Great's state apartments has an abstract modern ceiling fresco by Hann Trier in place of the original decor, which was destroyed by fire. Trier also painted the ceiling of the **Weiße Saal** (throne room and banquet hall).

Schloss Charlottenburg

The finest achievement of Knobelsdorff at Schloss Charlottenburg is the 42m (138ft) -long **Goldene Galerie**. This rococo ballroom, with its marble walls and gilded stucco, leads to two rooms containing a fine group of **Watteau paintings**. Frederick the Great was somewhat amused by the French artist's insolent *Enseigne du Gersaint*, a shop sign for art dealer Gersaint, in which a portrait of Louis XIV is being unceremoniously packed away. Among various other fine works by Watteau, you will find *L'amour paisible* (Quiet Love) and *Les Bergers* (The Shepherds).

When it is time for a break or lunch, make for the **Kleine Orangerie**, then head off to explore the **Schlosspark**. Among the many buildings in the grounds, nearest to the palace is the Italian-style **Neuer Pavillon**, built in 1825 according to plans by Karl Friedrich Schinkel. North of the carp pond, the elegant **Belvedere**, once a teahouse, now contains a collection of exquisite 18th- and 19th-century porcelain. Also worth visiting in the park is Queen Louise's mausoleum with her marble sarcophagus inside. At Schlossbrücke, behind the palace, is a landing point for pleasure boats taking river cruises to the new government quarter and Alexanderplatz.

The Langhansbau west of the palace was constructed as a theatre and once housed the Museum of Prehistory and Early History, which is now ensconced in the Neues Museum on Museum Island.

Opposite the palace are the two so-called 'Stüler buildings'. The western one is the home of the **Museum Berggruen** (www. smb.museum; Tue–Sun 10am–6pm; charge), an outstanding collection of late 19th- and early 20th-century art assembled by the Berlin-born collector Heinz Berggruen (1914–2007). There are works by many of the great masters of Modernism, while the heart of the collection is formed by dozens of pieces by Picasso. The eastern building is home to the **Sammlung**

Scharf-Gerstenberg (Tue–Sun 10am–6pm; charge), a collection of Surrealist art. The collection includes paintings, sculptures and drawings by artists such as Goya, Klinger, Redon, Dalí, Magritte, Ernst and Klee. The art is accompanied by a film programme that includes the classic Surrealist films of Salvador Dalí and Luis Buñuel, as well as films by contemporary artists who draw upon Surrealism.

The private **Bröhan Museum** (www.broehan-museum.de; Tue–Sun 10am–6pm; charge), dedicated to Art Nouveau and Art Deco, is housed in a former infantry barracks opposite the eastern Stüler building. Its

Statue in the grounds of the palace

peaceful interior makes a fine setting for the array of elegant objects amassed by businessman Karl Bröhan from the 1960s onwards. Highlights include superb ceramics, glassware, silverware and furniture.

OLYMPIC STADIUM

Built for the Games of 1936, Hitler's **Olympiastadion** ㉚ (www.olympiastadion-berlin.de) was spared bombardment, to serve as headquarters for the British Army. The structure's bombastic gigantism is an eloquent testimony to the Führer's taste in architecture. Viewed from the main Olympic Gate, it appears surprisingly 'low slung' until you see that the field itself has been sunk 12m (40ft) below ground level. The 74,000-capacity stadium still stages sporting events, and is open daily to the public at other times (9am–8pm in summer, 10am–4pm in winter). The stadium was modernised in 2006 in preparation for the football World Cup.

West of the stadium, the **Glockenturm** (bell tower) gives a magnificent view over the Olympic site. Beyond the tower, a pathway leads to the **Waldbühne**, an open-air amphitheatre, which is a summer venue for pop and classical concerts.

On Messedamm, southeast of the stadium, stands another colossus, the famous **ICC** (International Congress Centre). One of the world's biggest convention centres, the complex is also used for staging cultural events. Next to it on the equally huge **Messe und Ausstellungsgelände** (Trade Fair and Exhibition Area), the **Funkturm** (Radio Tower) is positively tiny; 150m (492ft) to the tip of its antenna, less than half the height of the Television Tower (see page 65). For breathtaking views, take the lift to the restaurant, 55m (180ft) up, or to the observation platform right at the top.

GEDENKSTÄTTE PLÖTZENSEE

Northeast of Charlottenburg, the **Gedenkstätte Plötzensee** ❸ in Hüttigpfad (daily Mar–Oct 9am–5pm, Nov–Feb until 4pm, www.gedenkstaette-ploetzensee.de) is a stark, moving memorial to the victims of Nazi persecution (take bus 123 from Turmstraße U-Bahn station). On the opposite side of the road a lane leads to the site of the prison where thousands of people were tortured and executed between 1933 and 1945, including many of the officers involved in the Stauffenberg plot to kill Hitler.

The dark sheds where executions were carried out have been preserved, and outside a stone urn, filled with soil from concentration camps, stands in a corner of the yard. In one

The Olympic Stadium

of the sheds you will find a small and poignant exhibition of historical documents, which includes death warrants and pictures of leading members of the German resistance. There is an information office where you can obtain free booklets in English, French and Russian.

DAHLEM

The history of leafy **Dahlem** ㉜ probably goes back for more than 750 years, and something of its rustic character remains, to which the thatched and half-timbered U-Bahn station makes a certain contribution. Opposite the station is one of Berlin's oldest buildings, a manor house dating back to 1560, which is part of the **Domäne Dahlem**, a visitor-friendly rural estate with old buildings, a museum, farm animals, well-tended fields, traditional crafts and carriage rides. Dahlem is also an academic and museum district; it was chosen as the site of the Free University set up during the 1948 Airlift as an alternative to the Humboldt University in the Soviet sector of the city, and it is home to some of Berlin's finest museums.

The main complex is known as the **Museen Dahlem** (Lansstraße 8; U-Bahn Dahlem-Dorf; www.smb.museum; Tue–Fri 10am–6pm, Sat–Sun 11am–6pm; charge). It consists of four museums housing a huge range of art and crafts from around the world. The **Museum für Ostasiatische Kunst** (Museum of East Asian Art) displays treasures from China, Japan and Korea, including delicate paper hangings, wooden screens, paintings, carpets, ceramics and lacquerware; and there is a room devoted to Buddhist art from all three countries. The **Museum für Indische Kunst** (Museum of Indian Art) is devoted to art and crafts from Pakistan, Afghanistan, Sri Lanka, Nepal, Tibet, Southeast Asia and Central Asia, and includes a fine selection of Buddhist sculpture.

The **Ethnologisches Museum** (Ethnological Museum) focuses on the cultures of ancient America, the South Seas, and South and East Asia, with a special section on Native North Americans and a spectacular presentation on art from Africa.

At the rear, the **Museum Europäischer Kulturen** (Arnimallee 25) deals with the folk culture of European peoples, with displays of tools, clothes, toys and much else.

The **Brücke-Museum** (Bus 115 to Pücklerstraße from U-Bahn Oskar-Helene-Heim, then 5 mins on foot; www.bruecke-museum.

Botanical garden

Berlin's superlative Botanischer Garten (Königin-Luise-Straße 6–8; S-Bahn Botanischer Garten; www. bgbm.org; 9am–dusk) is also in Dahlem. Its tropical houses contain some 18,000 species of exotic plants and there is also a smell and touch garden for the blind. A small museum at the north entrance covers the history and use of plants.

de; Wed–Mon 11am–5pm; charge) houses a number of fine works by early 20th-century German artists. It was founded in 1967 thanks to the legacy of Karl Schmidt-Rottluff, a member of the Expressionist group *Die Brücke*, which worked in Dresden from 1905 to 1913. A large number of the group's works were labelled as 'degenerate' and thus destroyed by the Nazis. Schmidt-Rottluff's own bold paintings hang beside the works of fellow Expressionists Emil Nolde, Erich Heckel, Ernst Ludwig Kirchner and Max Pechstein.

Museen Dahlem

GRUNEWALD AND WANNSEE

On the western edge of Berlin, the dense pine forest, which was largely stripped for fuel in 1945, has been replanted, adding to the 18 million pines around six million chestnut, linden, beech, birch and oak trees. The lush wooded areas form a reserve for deer, wild boar, marten, fox and rabbits, but there are also plenty of green meadows for picnics, and the forest paths are extremely popular with both cyclists and joggers.

The easiest and most direct way to get to the Grunewald is to take the S-Bahn from Bahnhof Zoo to Grunewald S-Bahn station. Alternatively, you could combine your trip with a visit to the museums at Dahlem; the Brücke Museum is only a 20-minute walk from the eastern edge of the forest. Drivers take the Avus and turn off on the Hüttenweg to **Grunewaldsee** ㉝, a lake offering swimming and sandy beaches. On the east shore, in an attractive lakeside setting of beech trees, you will find the **Jagdschloss Grunewald**, a hunting lodge built in 1542 for Prince Elector Joachim II. Situated in a cobbled courtyard, the lodge has been restored to its original Renaissance appearance. Inside you'll find an exhibition about Berlin portrait painting throughout the centuries, as well as a collection of early German hunting portraits and landscapes, which includes a series of panels depicting the Passion Cycle by Lucas Cranach, as well as works by Jordaens, Rubens and Bruyn.

On the Grunewald's west side, along Havelchaussee, the **Grunewaldturm** (Grunewald Tower) is a neo-Gothic tower built in 1897 to commemorate the 100th anniversary of the birth of Wilhelm I. A restaurant at the foot of the tower is

TEUFELSBERG – DEVIL'S MOUNTAIN

At the beginning of the Grunewald, in the middle of the flat, northern European plain that stretches from Warsaw to the Netherlands, is a mountain. Aptly named Teufelsberg (Devil's Mountain), it is not tall – only 115m (380ft) – but a mountain nevertheless, painstakingly created from a pile of rubble left by World War II bombardments.

In summer, the hill is grassed over for toddler mountain climbers to scramble around on. In winter, snow creates an excellent toboggan run, a good nursery slope for skiers, and even two bone-rattling ski jumps. The flatness of the north European plain east of the mountain is demonstrated by the summit where military radar equipment used to scan as far as Asia.

open daily from 10am. Ferry stations in the area offer boat rides on the River Havel and forest lakes, and the east bank of the Havel is lined with sandy beaches as far as the Wannsee lakes.

The waterfront near **Wannsee** ❸❹ S-Bahn station is a crowded spot where city-dwellers let their hair down on warm spring and summer days. The water bustles with pleasure boats and ferries, and you can cruise all the way to Potsdam from here. **Strandbad Wannsee** is Berlin's biggest beach, and the longest one in inland Europe.

Jagdschloss Grunewald

To the west of the Großer Wannsee, Königstraße crosses Berliner Forst, an extension of the Grunewald to **Glienicke Park**. Its whimsical landscaping of little hills, bridges and ponds was the work of Peter Josef Lenné in the early 19th century. **Schloss Glienicke** (1828) is a rather austere neoclassical edifice, but the nearby cloister, villa and garden houses add a romantic touch.

A ferry links **Pfaueninsel** ❸❺ (Peacock Island), a delightfully tranquil nature reserve in the Havel, to the northern edge of Berliner Forst. The island menagerie was used to stock the Berlin Zoo, but the bird sanctuary still has much to offer the nature-lover, including peacocks of course.

At the southern tip, half hidden in the trees, is Schinkel's Swiss Cottage, but the island's principal curiosity is the

Schloss Pfaueninsel folly, built in 1797 as a hideaway for Friedrich Wilhelm II and his lover, the Countess Wilhelmine von Lichtenau. The white wooden facade imitates granite blocks, and the turrets are joined together at the top by a pretty bridge.

Königsstraße extends as far as an illustrious relic of the Cold War, **Glienicker Bridge**, once a restricted border crossing between West Berlin and East Germany, where the KGB and CIA exchanged spies.

TEMPELHOF

A working terminal until 2008, Tempelhof Airport (U-Bahn Platz der Luftbrücke; www.tempelhoferfreiheit.de; dawn–dusk, tours Sat 3pm, Sun 2pm; grounds free, charge for tour) to the south of the city centre is an intriguing piece of Berlin's history, which can be visited on a fascinating guided tour. Rebuilt in typically stern National Socialist style in the late 1920s, this once vibrant aerodrome was Berlin's main hub during the Nazi era, but was taken over by the US Army in 1945. Probably its finest hour was during the Berlin airlift when the airport buildings were used as the air bridge operations base. The US Air Force was based here during the Cold War, but when the Wall came down the Americans left and the city chose Schönefeld as its main commercial airport. A must for aviation and history fans alike.

POTSDAM

A visit to the elegant old Baroque town of Potsdam comes highly recommended. A much older settlement than Berlin (it was first mentioned as Poztupimi in AD993), it is situated 30km (19 miles) southwest of the city. You can get there from central Berlin in a number of ways, of which the quickest is by Regional Express train from Bahnhof Zoo to Potsdam Hauptbahnhof. S-Bahn Line 7 also runs to Wannsee where you can change onto the S1 for Potsdam Hauptbahnhof. From Potsdam Hauptbahnhof, visitors heading straight for Sanssouci should take the 695 bus.

SANSSOUCI

Potsdam's main attractions are the summer palaces and gardens at Sanssouci, built in the 18th and 19th centuries. The vast grounds are filled with charming palaces, pavilions, fountains and temples. **Schloss Sanssouci** 36 (www.spsg.de; Tue–Sun 10am–6pm, 5pm in winter; charge) was commissioned by Frederick the Great and designed by von

The Glienicker Bridge

Knobelsdorff in 1744 from the king's own sketches. Despite only being single-storey, the 97m (300ft) -long garden front is very impressive, with its floor-to-ceiling windows and 35 huge caryatids supporting the roof and dome architrave. Highlights of the magnificent rococo interior include Frederick's splendid **Konzertsaal** (Concert Chamber) where walls and ceiling are overlaid with delicate gilt filigree; at the centre of the palace, beneath the dome, the **Marmorsaal** (Marble Hall) contains exquisite columns made from Carrara marble and stucco figures on the cornice. Among the guest rooms, the yellow **Voltaire room** is home to some bizarre decorations including wooden parrots hanging from perches.

Nearby, the **Bildergalerie** (Picture Gallery, closed in winter)

was designed to house Frederick the Great's collection of paintings by masters such as Caravaggio and Rubens.

A path through the woods southwest of the palace leads to the **Chinesisches Haus** (Chinese House, closed in winter). On top sits a gilded mandarin under a sunshade; inside you will find a collection of Chinese porcelain.

At the far western end of the Hauptallee stands the **Neues Palais** (New Palace), a vast structure built in the 1760s and covered in rococo statuary. It contains a rich collection of furniture, paintings by Italian, Dutch and French Baroque and rococo masters, and some fine 18th-century ceiling frescoes.

Other highlights of the park include the **Römische Bäder** (Roman Baths) by Schinkel, and **Schloss Charlottenhof**. To the north is the vast Italian Renaissance-style **Orangerie**.

SCHLOSS CECILIENHOF

Beside a lake, north of the town centre, is **Neuer Garten**, a pleasant English-style park. It contains **Schloss Cecilienhof**, the half-timbered pastiche of an English country manor built for Crown Prince Wilhelm and his wife. Winston Churchill, Joseph Stalin and Harry Truman met here in July 1945 to draw up the Potsdam Agreement, which defined how Germany was to be divided for the next 45 years. Today it is a luxury hotel and museum (Tue–Sun 10am–6pm, 5pm in winter).

TOWN CENTRE ATTRACTIONS

Arriving in Potsdam by boat or train, the first major building you will see is the neoclassical **Nikolaikirche**. Designed by Karl-Friedrich Schinkel, its dome bears a striking resemblance to that of St Paul's Cathedral in London. Opposite, on the other side of the Havel, stands the Baroque Town Hall. The old town has three historic gates, the Brandenburger Tor, the Jägertor and the Nauenertor; beyond the latter lies the

The garden front of Schloss Sanssouci

attractive **Holländische Viertel** (Dutch quarter), built for Dutch settlers between 1734 and 1741 by Jan Boumann.

EINSTEIN TOWER
To the south of the town centre, Albert-Einstein-Straße climbs Telegrafenberg to the bizarre **Einsteinturm**, built in 1921 as an astrophysics observatory. Albert Einstein was present here at a memorable technical demonstration of his Theory of Relativity. The observatory is still in use and, for want of a fitting statue to the great man, staff have placed in the entrance hall, as a splendidly atrocious visual pun, a simple small stone – Ein Stein.

BABELSBERG
Babelsberg was home to the German film industry, which rivalled Hollywood in the 1920s. Now run as a studio and theme park, **Filmpark Babelsberg** (www.filmpark-babelsberg.de; Apr–Oct daily 10am–6pm; charge) organises tours.

WHAT TO DO

In this liveliest of German cities, there is no lack of activities once your sightseeing is done; Berlin has never relinquished its role as the country's capital of the arts or shopping.

ENTERTAINMENT

Berliners are assiduous concert- and theatre-goers, so plan ahead if you want good tickets for the main events. Ask at a travel agency or tourist office about upcoming programmes, and book in advance where possible. In addition to the monthly publication *Berlin Programm*, there are two listings magazines, *Tip* (www.tip-berlin.de) and *Zitty* (www.zitty. de), published every two weeks, which give full details and reviews. *The Exberliner* (www.exberliner.com, with English online ticket shop) is Berlin's English-language paper, published monthly. Tickets and information are also available on the Berlin Tourism Organisation's website: www.visitberlin.de.

MUSIC

Symphonic music in Berlin centres on the Berliner Philharmoniker, one of the world's greatest orchestras, with Sir Simon Rattle as chief conductor. It is housed in the Philharmonie (see page 45). Other renowned orchestras also perform there, such as the Berliner Staatskapelle under Daniel Barenboim, and the Deutsches Symphonie-Orchester Berlin. Schinkel's beautifully restored Schauspielhaus on Gendarmenmarkt (known as the Konzerthaus Berlin, see page 57) is another important venue for classical music performances.

Chamber music and *Lieder* (song) recitals take place in the Kammermusiksaal (at the rear of the Philharmonie) and the Universität der Künste, Hardenbergstraße 33.

The striking Philharmonie, home of the Berlin Philharmonic

Berlin's **opera** lovers are well served by the Deutsche Oper in Bismarckstraße, the Staatsoper Unter den Linden (performing at the Schiller Theater in Charlottenburg until October 2017) and the Komische Oper in Behrenstraße.

Major **rock** concerts are usually performed at large venues such as the O2 World Arena, Max-Schmeling-Halle, the Velodrom, the open-air Waldbühne and the Olympic Stadium. **Jazz** is particularly popular in Berlin. Venues include Quasimodo (Kantstraße 12a; www.quasimodo.de) and A-Trane Jazzclub (Bleibtreustraße 1; www.a-trane.de). Jazzfest Berlin is an annual jazz festival held in early November.

THEATRE AND CINEMA

Berlin boasts over 150 theatres, and even without a great command of the language any enthusiastic theatregoer can enjoy some memorable and stirring performances.

The city's most controversial theatre performances are staged at the Volksbühne (Rosa-Luxemburg-Platz), while the Schaubühne (Lehniner Platz on Ku'damm) achieved international renown for its classical avant-garde and experimental theatre. The plays of Berlin's best-known playwright, Bertolt Brecht, are still performed at the theatre he founded, the Berliner Ensemble (Bertolt-Brecht-Platz 1; www.berliner-ensemble.de). **Contemporary plays** are staged at the Maxim-Gorki-Theater (Am Festungsgraben 2; www.gorki.de), and the **classics** at the Deutsches Theater (Schumannstraße 13a; www.deutschestheater.de). The English Theatre Berlin (Kreuzberg, Fidicinstraße 40; www.etberlin.de) offers a wide variety of quality English-language theatre.

For **popular theatre,** such as musicals, operettas and comedies, try the Theater des Westens (Kantstraße 12) and the

Musical Theater (Marlene-Dietrich-Platz 1), as well as the Admiralspalast (Friedrichstraße 101).

Berlin's largest audience magnet is the **Friedrichstadtpalast** (www.show-palace.eu) the only revue theatre in Germany and the largest in Europe. Each production is produced exclusively and performed by the house troupe and orchestra.

As befits a city that every February hosts a major international film festival, Berlin is endowed with a huge number of **cinemas**. Most foreign-language films are dubbed into German, though some cinemas will show films in the original language (*Originalfassung* – OF).

CABARET

Another long-standing tradition, at its heyday in the 1920s, satirical cabaret has always, by its very nature, had to

Staatsoper Unter den Linden

struggle for existence. Survivors among countless fly-by-nights include *Die Stachelschweine* (Europa-Center) and *Die Distel* (Friedrichstraße 101). However, unless your German is excellent, this cabaret will be almost impossible to follow. Bar jeder Vernunft (Schaperstraße 24) and Tipi (close to the Chancellery) offer more music-orientated programmes.

Transvestite shows are a feature of Berlin and can be saucy, often witty, and occasionally outrageous. Long-established **Cabaret Chez Nous** (Marburger Straße 14) tries to evoke the frivolity of the 1920s. A more family-friendly show – a mix of juggling, aerial acrobatics, comedy and slapstick – is to be enjoyed at **Chamäleon Variete** (Hackesche Höfe; www.chamaeleon berlin.com).

Night lights at the Sony Center

CLUBS AND BARS

Known for its round-the-clock, open-end partying, Berlin has hundreds of venues to choose from. Saturday night parties rarely get going before 1am. In summer, beach bars along the River Spree attract the crowds.

Berlin has several night-life hotspots, one of which is Prenzlauer Berg. A good place to start is **Kulturbrauerei** (Schönhauser Allee 36/Sredzkistraße; www.kultur brauerei.de), a complex of bars, restaurants and theatres on the renovated grounds of an old brewery, offering a vibrant mix of art, music and entertainment. It always draws a crowd.

As the night goes on, choices are limitless. In Mitte, try **Clärchens Ballhaus** (Auguststraße 24; www.ballhaus.de), an old-worldly dancehall where Berliners of all ages and walks of life meet to dance the night away. A contrasting venue is **Felix** (Behrenstraße 72; www.felix-clubrestaurant.de), an exclusive club and lounge restaurant located at the back of the Hotel Adlon, frequented by celebrities and wannabes alike. **Weekend Club Berlin** (Alexanderplatz 5; www.week-end-berlin.de) is a two-floor house and techno club on the 13th floor of a Soviet-style block, with a welcoming atmosphere and a roof terrace. Over on Köpenicker Straße are legendary **Tresor** (www.tresorberlin.com), at No. 70 in an old power plant, and at No. 76 the **Sage Club** (www.sage-club.de), which hosts notorious KitKatClub parties at weekends and has three dance floors, a special pool area and a fire-breathing dragon.

In Friedrichshain try **Maria am Ostbahnhof** (Stralauer Platz 34-35, on the riverbank near Ostbahnhof station; www.club maria.de), with its electronic-leaning live acts and relaxed, unpretentious atmosphere. **Berghain** (Am Wriezener Bahnhof 1; www.berghain.de), with its high-energy music, is another popular hotspot.

In neighbouring Kreuzberg, a traditional hangout, try **Junction Bar** (Gneisenaustraße 18, near U7 stop Gneisenaustraße; www. junction-bar.de), a basement club with live music until DJs take over later in the night. There's a relaxed atmosphere and affordable drinks. A much sleeker venue is **Solar** (Stresemannstraße 76, through a back alley to the glass lift behind the car park, www.solarberlin.com), a 17th-floor bar-lounge near Potsdamer Platz that combines spectacular views (get there before sunset) with a fashionable interior and well-mixed drinks. Also in Kreuzberg, the place to chill after a long weekend of partying is

Club der Visionäre (Am Flutgraben 1, www.clubdervisionaere. com). Young Berliners relax on boats and floats moored on a canal near Schlesisches Tor underground station.

SHOPPING
WHERE TO SHOP

Each of Berlin's many districts has its own shopping area, but the city's retail heart remains in the west, on and around the Kurfürstendamm. The Ku'damm itself is lined with trendy boutiques and large department stores such as **Karstadt.** The most famous international designer labels and some exquisite jewellers have luxurious stores on the Ku'damm, particularly between Bleibtreustraße and Olivaer Platz. The cherished institution of **KaDeWe** on Wittenbergplatz, the **Europa-Center** multi-storey mall and the redeveloped **Kranzler Eck** with its striking glass skyscraper are close at hand, while elegant shopping streets lead off to the north and south, with a particular focus around Savignyplatz.

In the east, shoppers crowd Friedrichstraße in search of designer labels. The complex of stylish malls known as the Friedrichstraße Passagen are always busy, and the glittering premises of **Galeries Lafayette** offer an injection of French style. The streets and courtyards north of **Hackescher Markt**

GIFT HUNTING IN MUSEUMS

Museum shops are great places to track down art posters, lithographs and high-quality reproductions. In museums of classical antiquity such as the Egyptian Museum and the Pergamonmuseum, you can buy excellent copies of Greek vases or ancient sculpture in bronze, plaster or resin. Museum shops also offer a certain guarantee of quality for genuine artisan products such as textiles, pottery, pewter and woodcarving.

have been colonised by a fascinating mixture of fashion boutiques, galleries, antique dealers and bookshops. At the junction of east and west, Potsdamer Platz boasts **Arkaden**, a large indoor shopping centre with 100-plus shops and supermarkets.

Most of the city's shops are open Monday to Saturday from 9 or 10am until 8pm. However, many outlets, especially in quiet neighbourhoods, may close earlier. Shops are allowed to open from 1–8pm on Sundays in Advent, and six other Sundays during the year.

Galeries Lafayette

WHAT TO BUY

Antiques. Any moderately priced furniture or porcelain that claims to be Baroque or rococo is probably a copy. Concentrate on items dating from the 19th and early 20th centuries. Some of the side streets off the Ku'damm (such as Fasanenstraße) are the best places to start.

Books. Big general bookshops like Hugendubel (in KaDeWe and at Tauentzienstraße 13) and Dussmann (Friedrichstraße 90) are lavishly stocked and have some English-language books. Marga Schoeller Bücherstube (Knesebeckstraße 33) has a small, interesting English section. Specialist English-language bookshops include Books in Berlin (Goethestraße 69; www.booksinberlin.de) and Village Voice (Ackerstraße 1a; www.villagevoice.de), which also has a café. The bookstore

Berlin Story (Unter den Linden 26; www.berlinstory.de) is devoted exclusively to 'Berlin' and offers about 300 English-language titles. The capital is also home to many second-hand and antiquarian bookshops, especially on Schlüterstraße and along Knesebeckstraße.

Bric-a-brac. Berlin has many flea markets (*flohmarkt* in German). Among the best is the Berliner Antik- und Flohmarkt located in the S-Bahn arches beneath Friedrichstraße station (closed Tue). A huge selection of second-hand records, *objets d'art* and clothes can be found at the weekend flea market

Wooden and handmade children's toys at Heidi's Spielzeugladen

on the Straße des 17. Juni in Charlottenburg. Another popular weekend flea market, specialising in art, books and records, is the one held on the Kupfergraben opposite the Museumsinsel. Head to the Turkish Market (*Türkischer Wochenmarkt*) on the Landwehr canal's Maybachufer in Kreuzberg for all manner of wares, as well as to try exotic food, and buy spices and utensils (open Tue and Fri afternoons).

Gourmet Delicacies. Among the pastries and cakes that travel best are *Lebkuchen* (gingerbread), *Spekulatius* (spiced Christmas cookies) and marzipan. KaDeWe's *Feinschmeckeretage* (gourmet floor) offers 500 different

breads and 1,500 different types of cheese, plus rare eastern delicacies, exotic teas, handmade chocolates and Beluga caviar.
Porcelain. Look for modern Rosenthal and the local Königliche Porzellan Manufaktur (KPM), which was launched by Frederick the Great in the 18th century. The KPM shop on the factory premises (at Wegelystraße 1 near Straße des 17. Juni) also sells reduced-price seconds. Other celebrated manufacturers represented in Berlin are Meissen (at Charlottenstraße 34), Nymphenburg of Munich and Frankenthal.

SPORTS

The lakes and rivers in and around Berlin provide endless opportunities for **watersports**. It is easy to rent equipment for waterskiing, canoeing, rowing, sailing and windsurfing. Swimmers have around 20 beaches at their disposal, most of them pleasantly sandy. Continuing the old Prussian devotion to physical culture, a few of the beaches are reserved for nude bathing – or FKK, as you may see it signposted. The most popular of these beaches are the Bullenwinkel on the Grunewaldsee, Strandbad Halensee and the Teufelssee. If you would rather wear a swimming costume, try the lovely beaches of the Wannsee, Glienicker See, the Havel, or the less crowded Großer Müggelsee, far in the east of Berlin, and Templiner See, out at Potsdam.

Alternatively, swimmers can head for the Schwimm- und Sprunghalle in Europasportpark (Paul-Heyse-Straße 26, Prenzlauer Berg) or the beautiful, ornate Stadtbad Neukölln. The 'Kinderbad Monbijou' in the park opposite the Bode-Museum is a safe pool for small children. Many luxury hotels have pools and spa facilities for recreation.

Berlin's sports facilities are second to none, thanks in large part to the huge programme of building that took place as part of the city's unsuccessful bid for the 2000 Olympics. There are over

Sailing on the Wannsee

1,500 sports venues in the city, most impressive of which are the Max-Schmeling-Halle and the Velodrom (both in the Prenzlauer Berg district).

Golf enthusiasts can get a round in at the Golf und Landclub Berlin-Wannsee Club (Golfweg 22, www.wannsee.de), as well as at the Golf Club Gatow (www.golfclubgatow.de) in Spandau.

You can have a go at **indoor climbing** under the supervision of professionals at Magic Mountain in Wedding (Böttgerstraße 20–26).

In summer you are likely to encounter a **beach volleyball** game in full swing (such as behind the East Side Gallery in Friedrichshain). Joining in is encouraged.

One surprise sport you may not have expected to practise in Berlin is **hang-gliding,** but it is, in fact, possible to throw yourself off the Teufelsberg, where you can also do a little **skiing** and **sledding** in winter (see page 78). However, you don't have to go in search of snow to ski or snowboard; Der Gletscher (The Glacier, www.der-gletscher.de) ski centre in Pankow has the longest indoor ski course in the world.

Roller skating has become a way of life in Berlin; every Sunday evening – weather permitting – up to 4,000 skaters take part in a two-hour skate through the streets and squares of the city centre.

The most pleasant and effective defence against the aggressiveness of some of the city's **bicycle** goers is to rent your own bike and join them.

SPECTATOR SPORTS

The ultimate event in professional football is the final of the football **World Cup**, which Berlin hosted in 2006; the Olympic Stadium underwent a massive refurbishment programme for the big day. The annual **Six Day Cycle Race** has been held every January since 1997 at the Velodrom, while the Max-Schmeling-Halle draws **basketball** fans by the thousands to see the home team, Alba Berlin, take on the opposition. International **tennis** tournaments are held at the Rot-Weiß Club. **'Trotter' horse races** are held at two sites, and last, but by no means least, the **Berlin Marathon** can be enjoyed from the side lines throughout the city every September.

CHILDREN'S BERLIN

Cycling through the Brandenburg Gate

Children are well catered for in Berlin, and many of the things you'll want to do – trips out to the Grunewald, city tours by canal – will also appeal to young ones.

Museums: Some of the city's museums are specifically intended for children, among them the **Kindermuseum 'Labyrinth'** with a whole range of interactive features, the **MachMit Museum** and the **Juniormuseum** of the **Ethnological Museum.** Other museums with definite child-appeal include the **Museum für Naturkunde** with its amazing dinosaur skeleton,

the **Puppentheater-Museum** offering a behind-the-scenes experience of puppets and marionettes, and the **Deutsches Technikmuseum,** especially the hands-on Spectrum section. At the **Domäne Dahlem** there are craftspeople to watch and animals to admire, while the **Museumsdorf Düppel** is a re-creation of a medieval village, also with craft and farming activities. There are animals aplenty in Berlin's two zoos, the Zoologischer Garten near the Ku'damm and the Tierpark in Friedrichsfelde.

Parks and play areas: Well-equipped and maintained play areas can be found all over the city, in local neighbourhoods and in the many parks. The finest is probably the **Britzer Garten** in Neukölln, with all the usual features plus pools, water playground, animals and a miniature railway. On rainy days you could try the more commercial **Jacks Fun World** (in Reinickendorf), which has go-karts, bungee-trampoline, bumper-boats and more.

Other attractions: Loxx Miniatur Welten, the world's largest digitally controlled model railway, puts the capital into miniature perspective (ALEXA shopping centre, Alexanderplatz). There is a Planetarium (Prenzlauer Allee 80, Prenzlauer Berg) and an impressive AquaDom and Sea Life Centre (Spandauer Straße 3, Mitte), while the Ufa-Fabrik (Viktoriastraße 13–18, Tempelhof) has a children's circus and a farmyard. The Blue Man Group, at the Bluemax Theater on Potsdamer Platz, appeals to older kids and their parents. On the way to Potsdam, the **Filmpark Babelsberg** (see page 83) will keep the family busy for a whole day.

Hertha Berlin

The Olympic Stadium is the home ground of Berlin's top football club, Hertha Berlin (www.herthabsc.de). Not as well-known as clubs like Bayern Munich, it nevertheless enjoys moderate success in the Bundesliga and (occasionally) in European competitions.

CALENDAR OF EVENTS

For the most up-to-date information on the city's festivals and arts calendar, consult the tourist office, the monthly *Berlin Programm* brochure or the local press.

January: *Berliner Neujahrslauf:* a 4km (2.4-mile) run through the city streets, starting at the Brandenburg Gate; *Sechs-Tage-Rennen*: six-day cycle race at the *Velodrom; Internationale Grüne Woche*: food and agriculture fair, with specialities from around the world.

February: *Internationale Filmfestspiele Berlin*: Berlin's International Film Festival, in early February, rivals those in Cannes and Venice.

March/April: *Festtage*: classical music festival usually held around Easter at the Staatsoper Unter den Linden (in Schillertheater).

May: *Theatertreffen*: a German-language theatre festival with productions from all over Germany, Austria and Switzerland. *Karneval der Kulturen*: three days of multi-cultural song and dance on the streets of Kreuzberg.

May–Sept: *MuseumsInselFestival*: nightly events (film, concerts, theatre) on three stages at the Museumsinsel, Kulturforum and Museen Dahlem.

June: open-air classical music concerts by the Berlin Philharmonic at the Waldbühne. *Christopher Street Day*: large gay and lesbian event with markets, food, performances. *Internationales Stadionfest (ISTAF)*: the Olympic Stadium hosts a major track and field event.

July/August: lots of open-air festivals throughout the city, from the Beer Festival to the Köpenicker Blues & Jazzfestival.

September/October: *Berlin Marathon; Musikfest Berlin*: a major international festival of orchestra and chamber music.

October/November: *Tag der Deutschen Einheit* (3 October): celebrations to commemorate German reunification; *Oktoberfest*: beer festival. *Jazzfest Berlin*.

December: *Weihnachtsmärkte*, including *Winterzauber* on Potsdamer Platz: traditional Christmas markets are held on Breitscheidplatz and throughout the city. New Year's Eve party at the Brandenburg Gate.

EATING OUT

A new German cuisine (Neue Deutsche Küche) has emerged in response to a demand for greater culinary refinement. Good old German dishes aren't being replaced by French imitations, but they are being prepared with a new lightness and imagination. Berlin also has a greater variety of cuisines than any other German city, offering everything from Japanese to Hungarian food.

WHEN TO EAT

Mealtimes are quite flexible in Berlin, and you can always find somewhere to eat at virtually any time of day or night. Breakfast (frühstück) generally consists of a selection of rolls, boiled eggs, cheese, muesli and honey, cold meats, fruit juices, quark (soft cheese), yoghurt, and either coffee or tea. In hotels it can be served from as early as 6am until 11am, while many cafés offer a selection of breakfasts from about 9 or 10am until as late as 6pm.

A popular tradition in many eateries is the morning buffet, frühstücksbuffet, where you help yourself from the counter to as much as you can eat for a fixed price. Berliners take lunch (mittagessen) less seriously than other Germans, probably because the presence of so many fast-food (imbiss) places leads to constant snacking. In the evening, restaurants tend to fill up early and you should reserve in advance for the better establishments.

WHERE TO EAT

Choices range from high-class restaurants and bourgeois gaststätten via the rather chic and arty bistro or café down to the popular kneipe, originally student slang for any corner bar or tavern where you can have a drink and a snack big enough to call a meal. All of these places spill out onto the streets and squares as soon as the weather is warm enough; when it is not, there are outdoor heaters.

Afternoon tea in Berlin

The *konditorei* (café/pastry shop) is in a separate category all of its own. In this bourgeois paradise, and armed with a newspaper attached to a rod, you can indulge in the great German tradition of *kaffee und kuchen*, enjoyed by all. As well as cakes and pastries, ice cream, coffee, tea, hot chocolate, fruit juices and even wines, most places also offer a few light snacks and salads to stave off the hunger pangs. Café Einstein on Unter den Linden is perhaps one of the best places to sit and have breakfast or sample something from a daily selection of cakes. And don't forget the gourmet floor of KaDeWe, where you can sample a dazzling assortment of delicious foods from across the globe (see page 37).

Cafés provide an excellent place to sit and watch the world rush by while you relax. You can order a cup of coffee and then sit for hours without feeling pressured to leave, but it's also possible to fill up in Berlin's cafés for just a few euros.

Brauhaus (literally brewery) or *bierkeller*, the old beer-halls, continue to thrive, and become *biergarten* in the parks. Good beer, food and company come as standard.

A menu (speisekarte) is displayed outside most restaurants. Besides the à la carte menu, there are generally one or more set menus (menü or gedeck), which usually work out as pretty good deals. The service charge (bedienung) as well as value-added tax (mwst) are usually included; a small tip is sometimes, but not always, expected.

SOUPS AND STARTERS

Appetisers (or starters) can be found listed on the menu under *vorspeisen, kleine ger-*

Relaxing in a biergarten

ichte or *kalte platten*. Soups (suppen) and stews (eintopfgerichte) are often very hearty; sometimes they can be enough for a whole meal. You can sample all the traditional German soups in Berlin. *Leberknödelsuppe* comes with spicy dumplings of flour, breadcrumbs, ox liver, onions, marjoram and garlic. Served at its best, *kartoffelsuppe* is a rich combination of potato, leeks, parsnips, celery and bacon, while *bohnensuppe* is a hearty concoction of several varieties of beans. The city's favourite, however, is plain old lentil soup (linsensuppe), best with bits of sausage in it.

Starters include *hackepeter*, the German version of steak tartare, and *soleier*, eggs pickled in brine (sole), then peeled and halved and seasoned with salt, pepper, paprika, vinegar and oil. They are generally eaten with the ubiquitous Berlin mustard – *mostrich*.

MAIN DISHES

Fish is served fresh from the River Havel. Try specialities like *havelaal grün*, eel boiled in a dill sauce, or *havelzander*, pike-perch served with *salzkartoffeln* (simple but surprisingly tasty boiled potatoes). This very humble vegetable is something of a Berlin obsession. One of the city's great gourmet delights is the *kartoffelpuffer*, a sort of potato pancake; *kartoffelsalat* (potato salad) is also popular.

The supreme Berlin delicacy is undoubtedly *eisbein mit sauerkraut und erbsenpüree* – pork knuckle on a purée of peas with sauerkraut prepared in white wine, juniper berries, caraway seeds and cloves. Add a generous dollop of mustard, as always. A little more humble, but just as fine, is *gebratene Leber*, also known as *Leber Berliner Art*, sautéed liver served with slices of apple and browned onion rings.

The original recipe for *Kasseler rippen*, or smoked pork chops, came not from the town of Kassel, but from a Berlin butcher by the name of Kassel. Berlin also claims as its own two world-famous sausages: the giant *bockwurst* (a type of boiled sausage), so named because a local butcher advertised it suspended between the mouths of two goats *(bock)*; and the Viennese sausage, or *wiener*, which was invented, so they say, in Berlin.

In this predominantly meat-oriented culture, vegetarians

Beelitzer Spargel

For seven weeks in May and June, Berlin (and most of Germany) goes bananas for *Beelitzer Spargel*, locally grown white asparagus served with boiled potatoes and melted butter or Hollandaise sauce, accompanied by smoked ham or Schnitzel.

may end up feeling rather excluded. The good news, however, is that most places now include vegetarian dishes on their menus. *Gemüsestrudel* (a type of vegetable strudel) is made from courgettes, onions, sweetcorn, peppers and broccoli in a spicy tomato sauce, and wrapped in flaky pastry. *Ofenkartoffel mit kräuterquark* (baked potato filled with herb-flavoured soft cheese) is also a filling standby. Be wary of ordering something that perhaps sounds as if it will be meat-free, for example potato or lentil soup, but which will often contain bacon *(speck)* or sausage.

DESSERTS

A very popular dessert is *Rote Grütze* (a delicious compote of raspberries, cherries and blackcurrants), generally served with *vanillesoße* (vanilla sauce). If you really want to stretch your waistline, indulge yourself in the German national orgy of Konditorei treats like *schwarzwälder kirschtorte*, the creamy cherry cake from the Black Forest; *apfelstrudel* from Vienna is another favourite dessert. Berliners also love *haselnuss-sahnetorte* (hazelnut cream cake), *käsekuchen* (cheesecake) and *pflaumenkuchen* (Dresden plum cake).

CURRYWURST

Possibly the most famous dish that Berlin has given the rest of the German-speaking world is the *currywurst*. 'Invented' in 1949, this popular belly filler is simply grilled sausage swimming in ketchup and sprinkled with mild curry powder (the curry powder was given to its inventor by British soldiers). Why this oddly non-Eastern European dish has remained such a beloved snack among Germany's young people in particular is a mystery, though it really does hit the spot when hunger strikes after a night out.

WHAT TO DRINK

Frederick the Great tried to produce wine at Potsdam and the resulting brew was terrible, but today many Berlin restaurants offer a first-class array of many fine German wines. The red wines cannot be compared in quality to the famous white Rieslings of the Rhine and Mosel valleys but, generally speaking, the whole family of German wines is very respectable.

Gourmet dining

The most highly regarded German wines are those of the Rheingau. Among the labels to look for are Schloss Johannisberger, Hattenheimer, Kloster Eberbacher, Steinberger and Rüdesheimer. If a celebration is on the cards, you won't go far wrong with a bottle of the champagne-like Sekt. The best of the Rhine Valley red wines come from Assmannshausen and Ingelheim. From Rheinhessen, try the great Niersteiner Domtal and Oppenheimer. Bottled in green glass to distinguish them from the brown Rhine bottles, the Mosel wines enjoy their own delicate reputation. The most celebrated among the varietals include the Bernkasteler, Piesporter, Graacher and the Zeltinger.

Berlin's most popular drink, however, is still beer – local Berliner Pilsner, Schultheiss and Kindl, or the best Dortmund and Bavarian brews. They are served *vom Fass*, on tap, or bottled in several varieties: *Export*, light and smooth; *Pils*, light and strong; and *Bock*, which is a dark, rich lager.

Berlin Beer Festival

On the first weekend in August a 1,600m (1-mile) -stretch of Karl-Marx-Allee is transformed into the world's longest beer garden with the arrival of the Berlin Beer Festival (www.bierfestival-berlin. de). Brewers from across Germany, as well as from the Czech Republic, Belgium and the UK, set up their stalls on the broad verges, and stages with live music and shows provide entertainment.

In the summer months, as a refreshing surprise, try the *Berliner Weiße*, a foaming draught beer served up in a huge bowl-like glass complete with a shot *(mit Schuss)* of raspberry syrup or liqueur, or perhaps with *Waldmeister* (green woodruff syrup).

Berliners also like the custom of 'chasing' the beer with a shot of Schnapps; any hard, clear alcohol made from potatoes, corn, barley, juniper, or another grain or berry that will distil into something to warm the cockles in the winter months.

The brandy *(weinbrand)* made in Germany is not bad, but the very strong fruit Schnapps which are distilled either from cherries *(kirschwasser)*, plums *(zwetschgenwasser)* or raspberries *(himbeergeist)* are much better and are worth sampling. Whatever your poison, 'cheers', or as the locals say '*prost!*'

TO HELP YOU ORDER

I'd like to reserve a table... **Ich möchte einen Tisch... reservieren.**

for two **für zwei Personen**

for this evening **für heute Abend**

A table for..., please. **Bitte einen Tisch für...**
I'd like... **Ich möchte...**
The bill, please. **Die Rechnung, bitte.**

MENU READER

aal eel
apfel apple
apfelsine orange
aufschnitt cold cuts
  (charcuterie)
barsch bass
blutwurst blood sausage
braten roast
brot bread
(hühnchen-) brust
  breast (of chicken)
dorsch cod
ei/eier egg/eggs
eierkuchen pancake
eis ice cream
erdbeeren strawberries
fisch fish
fleisch meat
gans goose
geflügel poultry
gemüse vegetable
heilbutt halibut
himbeere raspberry
hummer lobster
kalb veal
kartoffel potato
käse cheese
kirsche cherry

klosse dumpling
knoblauch garlic
kuchen pie
lachs salmon
lamm lamb
lendenfilet sirloin
milch milk
paprikaschote pepper
  (vegetable)
pfirsich peach
pflaume plum
pilz mushroom
rinderbraten roast beef
rindfleisch beef
salat salad
salz salt
schinken ham
schweinefleisch pork
seeteufel monkfish
suppe soup
tee tea
thunfisch tuna
truthahn turkey
wasser water
wein wine
weintrauben grapes
wild game/venison
zwiebel onion

PLACES TO EAT

As a basic guide, we have used the following symbols to give an idea of the price for a three-course meal for one, including a service charge of 15 percent, but excluding wine:

€€€ over 50 euros   **€€** 30–50 euros   **€** below 30 euros

BERLIN CITY, WEST

Restaurant 44 €€€ *Augsburger Straße 44, at Swissôtel Berlin, tel: 220 102 288, www.swissotel.com.* Savour creative and innovative Swiss cuisine at this stylish restaurant with a roof terrace overlooking the Ku'damm. The menu features extravagant dishes that reflect tradition (regional cuisine) and evolution (avant-garde cuisine). Guests are seated among the fragrant herbs and spices cultivated in the roof garden. Reservations recommended. Monday–Friday 6–10.30am, 6–10.30pm, Saturday 7am–noon, 6–10.30pm, Sunday 7am–noon.

Alt Luxemburg €€€ *Windscheidstraße 31 (not far from U2 stop Sophie-Charlotte-Platz), tel: 323 87 30, www.alt-luxemburg.de.* Excellent cuisine with a French touch, served in a tasteful ambience. The desserts are among the best in Berlin. Reservations are strongly advised. Open Monday–Saturday 5pm–1am.

Diekmann €€€ *Meinekestraße 7, tel: 883 33 21, www.diekmann-restaurants.de.* This restaurant's interior looks like an old-fashioned store. The German-French-style dishes are cooked with ingredients fresh from Brandenburg's fields, woods and waters. Open Monday–Saturday noon–1am, Sunday and holidays 6pm–1am.

Don Quijote €€ *Bleibtreustraße 41 (near Savignyplatz S-Bahn stop), tel: 881 32 08.* This lively, long-established Spanish restaurant is notable for its excellent food, and has a friendly atmosphere. Open daily 4pm–1am. No credit cards.

Eiffel €€ *Ku'damm 105 (western end of the avenue), tel: 891 13 05.* As the name implies, this is a French restaurant, though definitely with a Mediterranean touch. The wood and steel interior is as sleek as the dishes on offer. Open daily 9am–2am.

First Floor €€€ *Budapester Straße 45, tel: 25 02 10 20*. www.first floorberlin.de. Michelin-starred gourmet cuisine is served in this elegant restaurant in the Hotel Palace. Open Tuesday–Saturday 6.30–11pm.

Florian €€ *Grolmanstraße 52, tel: 313 91 84*, www.restaurant-florian.de. Noisy, intellectual chic place in the fashionable area around Savignyplatz, serving solid southern German cuisine. Open daily 6pm–3am. No credit cards.

Istanbul €€ *Pestalozzistraße 84, tel: 883 27 77*. Extensive menu offering a choice of scrumptious Turkish fare, including some vegetarian starters. Belly dancing on Friday and Saturday nights. Open daily 10am–midnight.

Kempinski-Grill €€€ *Kurfürstendamm 27, tel: 88 43 40*, www.kempinski.com. Luxurious restaurant inside the Kempinski Hotel Bristol (see page 134). Alternatively, try the more informal Reinhard's im Kempinski, which serves regional specialities and has a lovely terrace. Open daily noon–1am.

Leibniz-Klause €€ *Leibnizstraße/Mommsenstraße 57, tel: 323 70 68*, www.leibniz-klause.de. Sophisticated and atmospheric pub-restaurant with a tempting range of local dishes. Open daily noon–1am.

Lutter & Wegner €€ *Charlottenstraße 56, tel: 202 95 415*. This elegant Berlin institution, which has been on the go since 1811, produces fresh, regional cuisine. Jazz music adds to the charm. Open daily 11am–3am.

Marjellchen €€ *Mommsenstraße 9 (two blocks from Savignyplatz), tel: 883 26 76*, www.marjellchen-berlin.de. Intimate, welcoming establishment specialising in unusual dishes from Germany's erstwhile eastern provinces, East and West Prussia, Pomerania and Silesia (now in Poland). Open daily 5pm–midnight.

Paris-Bar €€ *Kantstraße 152 (near Zoologischer Garten station),* *tel: 313 80 52.* Classic French and international cuisine in intellectual/arty atmosphere. A Berlin institution. Open daily noon–1am.

La Sepia €€ *Marburger Straße 2 (not far from Europa-Center),* *tel: 213 55 85.* www.lasepia-berlin.de. This cosy Spanish-Portuguese restaurant specialises in tapas and fish dishes, mainly grilled. Has a great, friendly atmosphere. Very reasonable lunch specials. Open Sunday–Thursday noon–midnight and Friday–Saturday noon–1am.

Wintergarten €€ *Fasanenstraße 23, tel: 882 54 14.* This haven of peace is situated in the Literaturhaus villa and is the perfect place to collect your thoughts after visiting the Käthe-Kollwitz-Museum nearby. The salon at the back is ideal on sunny days; in summer the garden doubles as an extra room. Open 9.30am–midnight. No credit cards.

KREUZBERG

Curry 36 € *Mehringdamm 36, tel: 251 7368.* Quintessentially postwar West Berlin, the *currywurst* (grilled sausage, doused in ketchup and sprinkled with curry powder) is as popular as ever and the best place to try a waxed tray of the stuff is this café near the Mehringdamm U-Bahn station. Open Monday–Sunday 9am–5pm.

Henne € *Leuschnerdamm 25 (four blocks from U8 Moritzplatz stop), tel: 614 77 30.* www.henne-berlin.de. Not that keen on chicken? Then you haven't tried the *milchmasthähnchen* (milk-fed chicken) here, almost the only fare on the menu. People flock to this unpretentious old Berlin *wirtshaus* for it. Reserve in advance. Open Tuesday–Saturday 6pm–1am, from 5pm Sunday.

Hostaria del Monte Croce €€ *Mittenwalder Straße 6 (near U7 Gneisenaustraße stop), tel: 694 39 68.* This tiny restaurant offers copious portions of genuine northern Italian food in an authentic atmosphere. Reserve in advance. Open for dinner only, from 7pm. Closed Sunday and Monday. No credit cards.

Osteria No. 1 €€ *Kreuzbergstraße 71 (near Victoriapark), tel: 786 91 62*. A lively ambience combined with good trattoria fare keep the regular young crowd flocking back for more. Inviting garden with playground. Reservations are highly recommended. Open daily noon–midnight. American Express and Visa only.

Sauvage Paleothek €€ *Pflügerstraße 25 (nearest U-Bahn is Hermannplatz), tel: 531 67 547, www.sauvageberlin.com*. Ever wondered what exactly people were eating 10,000 years ago? Find out at Berlin's first Palaeolithic restaurant, where surprisingly tasty meals are concocted using just fish, meat, eggs, seeds, nuts, fruit and vegetables native to Europe. Ingredients are organic. Tuesday–Sunday 6–11pm. There's also a big Paleo Sauvage Restaurant on *Winsstraße 30*, tel: 381 000 25, Wednesday–Sunday 6pm–midnight, Saturday and Sunday also 11.30am–3.30pm.

MITTE

Berliner Republik und Brokers Bierbörse € *Schiffbauerdamm 8 (at Friedrichstraße station, western exit), tel: 30 87 22 93, www.die-berliner-republik.de*. Big and breezy beer hall on the banks of the River Spree. As well as a good choice of solidly unpretentious food, there is an amazing range of beers, the prices of which go up and down on a screen as the demand fluctuates. Open 10am–6am. No credit cards.

Borchardt €€€ *Französische Straße 47 (off Gendarmenmarkt), tel: 81 88 62 62, www.borchardt-restaurant.de*. An elegant, airy restaurant with a 1920s atmosphere, conveniently situated just off the historic Gendarmenmarkt. The menu changes daily, portions are generous but service can occasionally leave something to be desired. Open daily 11.30am–1am.

Brechts €€ *Schiffbauerdamm 6–7 (near Friedrichstraße station, western exit)*, tel: 28 59 85 85, www.brechts.de. Located close to Bertolt Brecht's theatre, the Berliner Ensemble, directly on the river Spree. Austrian and international cuisine of high quality is plated up with skill and perfection. Open daily 11.30am–1am.

Dressler €€ *Unter den Linden 39*, tel: 204 44 22, www.restaurant-dressler.de. Art Deco style abounds in this sophisticated establishment, which is styled on the great restaurants of the 1920s and serves international cuisine. There is also a sister restaurant, by the same name, at Ku'damm 207–208 (tel: 883 35 30). Both are open daily 8am–1am.

Käfer Dachgarten Restaurant im Reichstag €€€ *Platz der Republik 1*, tel: 22 62 990. www.feinkost-kaefer.de. Reserving a table in this restaurant, run by Munich deli impresario Feinkost Käfer, is a great way to bypass the long Reichstag cupola queues. The fine meals come with a spectacular view. Bring your passport to get into the building. Open daily 9am–4.30pm, 6.30pm–midnight.

Reinhard's €€ *Poststraße 28*, tel: 242 52 95, www.reinhards.de. In the renovated Nikolaiviertel, this lively bistro, decorated in 1920s style, serves stylish cuisine to a mainly business clientele. Open daily 9am–midnight.

Ständige Vertretung € *Schiffbauerdamm 8*, tel: 282 39 65. Next door to the Berliner Republik, this cheerful establishment has an intriguing political theme, with photos, posters and much else decorating the walls. Serving typical Rhineland dishes and hoppy kölsch beer from Cologne, it's a welcoming home from home for politicians and civil servants exiled from the former seat of government in Bonn. Open daily 10.30am–1am.

Unsicht-Bar Berlin €€€ *Gormannstraße 14 (north of U8 Weinmeisterstraße stop)*, tel: 24 34 25 00, www.unsicht-bar-berlin.de. The food here is served in complete darkness by blind waiting staff. The idea is that removing sight gives your other senses – including taste – the chance to take over. Open

Wednesday–Thursday, Sunday 6pm–1am, from 5pm Friday–Saturday. Reservations requested.

Vau €€€ *Jägerstraße 54–55 (off Gendarmenmarkt), tel: 20 29 730*, www.vau-berlin.de. Elegant, unpretentious establishment serving outstanding regional and international cuisine. The service is friendly, and there is a small courtyard for pleasant lunches outside in the summer. Open Monday–Saturday noon–2.30pm, 7.30–10.30pm. Mastercard not accepted.

Weihenstephaner €€ *Neue Promenade 5, tel: 84 71 07 60*, www.weihenstephaner-berlin.de. Part of the Weihenstephaner brewery, this eatery on the square next to Hackescher Markt has *dirndl*-clad waitresses and serves hearty and satisfying Bavarian specialities. Open daily 11am–11pm.

Zur Letzten Instanz €€ *Waisenstraße 14–16 (near U2 stop Klosterstraße), tel: 242 55 28*. Berlin's oldest restaurant, founded in 1621, serves delicious regional cuisine and offers great set menus or buffets for travel groups. Open Tuesday–Saturday noon–1am.

FURTHER AFIELD

Altes Zollhaus €€ *Carl-Herz-Ufer 30, Kreuzberg, tel: 6923 300*, www.altes-zollhaus-berlin.de. New German cuisine is served in an idyllic green setting on the bank of the old Landwehrkanal. The timber-framed rustic building even has its own boat-landing, while the innovative cooking (the duck is splendid) was deemed worthy of a Gault Millau guide toque. Open Tuesday–Saturday 6pm–1am.

Blockhaus Nikolskoe €€ *Nikolskoer Weg, Wannsee, tel: 805 29 14*. Classic German cuisine in an old dacha originally built for Tsar Nicholas I, in a lovely setting overlooking the Havel and Peacock Island. Open daily 10.30am–6pm.

Café Einstein € *Kurfürstenstraße 58 (north of U1, 2, 3, 4 stop Nollendorfplatz), tel: 263 9190*, www.cafeeinstein.com. This Viennese-style coffeehouse provides international newspapers that you can read in a delightfully literary ambience while enjoying the freshly roasted coffee and the outstanding selection of mouth-watering cakes. There is also a branch in Unter den Linden. Open daily 8am–midnight. No credit cards.

Pasternak € *Knaackstraße 22–24 (near U2 stop Senefelderplatz), tel: 441 33 99*, www.restaurant-pasternak.de. In the trendy neighbourhood of Prenzlauer Berg, this restaurant plates up typical Russian fare to a mixed crowd of artists and intellectuals revelling in its authentic atmosphere. Open daily 9am–1am. Free Wi-fi 10am–6pm. No credit cards.

Probiermahl €€ *Dortmunder Straße 9 (in Moabit, west of Hansaviertel), tel: 399 69 69*, www.probiermahl.de. This popular restaurant serves small portions of food, allowing you to sample several dishes in a lively, sophisticated atmosphere. Excellent cocktails and a great place to watch beautiful people. Open Monday–Saturday 4pm–1am and Sunday 10am–midnight. Dinner served until 11.30pm.

Restauration 1900 €€ *Husemannstraße 1 (near Kollwitzplatz and Kulturbrauerei), tel: 442 24 94*. International cuisine predominates in this select restaurant in the heart of Prenzlauer Berg, which was a favourite even before the Wall came down. Commendable vegetarian selection, good wine list and attentive service. Reservations essential. Open daily from 10am.

Udagawa €€ *Feuerbachstraße 24, Steglitz (near S1 station Feuerbachstraße), tel: 792 23 73*, www.restaurant-udagawa.com. Excellent Japanese cuisine, especially the seafood options. Reservations essential. Open Wednesday–Monday 5.30–10.30pm.

Weinstein €€ *Lychener Straße 33 (near U2 stop Eberswalder Straße), tel: 441 18 42*. The charming ambiance of this wine tavern makes it a place for very special occasions. Delicious regional food, personal service and an unparalleled selection of German wines. Open Monday–Saturday 5pm–2am, Sunday 6pm–2am.

A–Z TRAVEL TIPS

A Summary of Practical Information

A

ACCOMMODATION (see also Camping and Recommended Hotels on page 133.

The Berlin Tourist Office publishes an English/German language list with full details of accommodation, ranging from the most expensive hotels to small guesthouses. The office also provides a reservation service, tel: 0049 (0)30 25 00 23 33; or contact them online at www.visitberlin.de. You can also inquire at the BERLIN infostores (www.visitberlin.de) at the Neues Kranzler Eck, Brandenburg Gate, Reichstag, Alexanderplatz, Hauptbahnhof or the Berlin-Brandenburg Tourist Information at Schönefeld Airport (see page 129). It is advisable but not crucial to book a month ahead.

I'd like a single/double room **Ich möchte bitte ein Einzel-/ Doppelzimmer**
with a bathroom/shower **mit Bad/Dusche**
How much per night/week? **Wie viel kostet es pro Nacht/ Woche?**

AIRPORTS

Berlin-Tegel, the gateway to Western Europe and New York, lies 8km (5 miles) northwest of the city centre. The best way into town is by express bus X9 to the bus station in front of Zoologischer Garten station or by express bus TXL to Unter den Linden. Two local buses call at U-Bahn stations: no. 109 to Zoologischer Garten stops at Jakob-Kaiser-Platz (two stops from the airport), and no. 128 to Osloer Straße stops at Kurt-Schumacher-Platz (five stops from the airport). A taxi from Tegel to Mitte costs around €30 and takes about 25 minutes.

Schönefeld Airport, which is mainly used for holiday flights, low-budget flights with airlines like easyJet and Ryanair, and flights to Eastern Europe and Asia, lies about 19km (12 miles) southeast of the city centre and is served by RE7 and RB14 red regional trains (fastest connection to the city) and S-Bahn. Lines S9 and S45 will take you to Alexanderplatz, from where bus, U- and S-Bahn connections to the rest of the city are plentiful. There is also the ExpressBus X7, connecting the airport with the underground station U Rudow (U-Bahn line 7). Taxi from Schönefeld to Mitte around €45 (about 35 minutes). **Brandenburg Airport** is due for completion in 2017 (www.berlin-airport.de).

Airport information. One telephone number covers airport information, tel: +49 (0)30 609 111 50 or www.berlin-airport.de.

Where can I get a taxi? **Wo finde ich ein Taxi?**
How much is it to the centre/Potsdamer Platz? **Wie viel kostet es ins Zentrum/zum Potsdamer Platz?**
Is this the bus to the Ku'damm? **Ist das der Bus nach zum Ku'damm?**

B

BICYCLE RENTAL

Bicycle lanes are usually marked by red bricks between the pavement and the road. Bikes are easy to rent; either look in the *Gelbe Seiten* (Yellow Pages) under *fahrradverleih*, or call 0180 510 8000 for information, or contact one of the following:

Fahrradstation, Friedrichstraße 95 (entrance Dorotheenstraße 30), tel: 20 45 45 00, open Mon–Fri 8am–7.30pm, Sat–Sun 10am–6pm.

Fahrradstation, Auguststraße 29, tel: 28 59 96 61, open Mon–Fri 10am–7.30pm and Sat 10am–6pm.

Fat Tire, Panoramastraße 1a (under the TV tower on Alexanderplatz), tel: 24 04 79 91, www.fattirebiketours.com, open daily 9am–8pm.

German Railways (DB) have also introduced a bike hire scheme, tel: 0700 05 22 55 22.

BUDGETING FOR YOUR TRIP

The following list will give you some idea of approximate prices to expect in Berlin. The sales tax for most goods and services (normally included) is 19 percent.

Buses, S-Bahn and U-Bahn, Trams. Tickets for public transport can be used interchangeably on buses,trams, S-Bahn and U-Bahn. One way ticket prices vary depending on the zones covered: AB €1.70, BC €2.10 and ABC is €2.40. See Transport on page 129 for more.

Entertainment. Cinema: €6–10.50, theatre: €11–38, club: €3–15.

Hotels (double room per night). Luxury class €250–450, first class €150–250, medium range €80–150, budget class €40–80. Hostels: beds in dorms from €9.50, typically €15–20, double rooms from €30.

Meals and drinks. Breakfast €5–20, lunch or dinner in fairly good establishment €20–45 (check out the lunch offers – *mittagstisch*), bottle of wine (German) €20–30, beer (half-litre) €3–4, soft drink (small bottle) €2–3, coffee €1.50–2.90.

Museums. Generally around €4–10, with reductions for students and free entrance to state museums for children under 16. The three-day Berlin Museum Pass (€24) offers admission to the museums on Museumsinsel, together with around 50 other museums in the city. Tickets are available from the Tourist Offices and museums. The Welcome Card (see page 130) provides reductions of up to 50 percent in entry prices for many major attractions, plus significant transport savings.

C

CAMPING

Campingplatz Am Krossinsee, Wernsdorfer Straße 38, Schmöckwitz, Berlin, tel: 675 86 87.

Campingplatz Breitehorn, Breitehornweg 24, Spandau, Berlin, tel: 365 34 08.

Campingplatz Bürgerablage, Niederneuendorfer Allee, Spandau, Berlin, tel: 335 45 84.

Campingplatz Kladow, Krampnitzer Weg 111–117, Spandau, Berlin, tel: 365 27 97.

City-Camping und Hotel, Gartenfelder Straße 1, Spandau, Berlin, tel: 33 50 36 33.

WohnmobilPark Berlin, Waidmannsluster Damm 12–14, Tegel, tel: 20 16 63 33.

Costs: tent €5–11 per person per night; caravan (trailer) €8–12 per person per night. For full information about campsites, visit www. visitberlin.de/en/book/overnight-stays/apartments-camping.

CAR HIRE (See also Driving)

By far the best way to hire a car is online before you leave home. You can also arrange to hire a car immediately upon arrival at Tegel or Schönefeld airports with one of the major international companies, though you'll pay for the pleasure. Otherwise refer to the yellow pages under *autovermietung* for leading companies. Average turn-up-and-drive costs: VW Polo €50 per day, BMW3 €80 per day.

To hire a car you'll need a valid driving licence held for at least one year and a credit card. The minimum age is 19, although some companies may have a higher minimum age.

All hire companies listed also have branches at the airports and at the Hauptbahnhof.

Avis, Budapester Straße 43, tel: 230 9370, www.avis.de.

Europcar, Alexanderplatz 8, tel: 240 79 00, www.europcar.de.

Hertz, Friedrichstraße 50–55, tel: 24 24 440, www.hertz.de.

Sixt, Budapester Straße 45, tel: 01805 252 525, www.sixt.de.

I'd like to rent a car **Ich möchte bitte ein Auto mieten**
...tomorrow **für morgen**
...for one day/week **für einen Tag/für eine Woche**
Please include full insurance. **Bitte schließen Sie eine Vollkaskoversicherung ab.**

CLIMATE

Berlin's climate follows the continental pattern of cold, snowy winters and agreeably warm summers with low humidity. The best time for a visit is late spring or summer when temperatures tend to be mild. Average temperatures are as follows:

	J	F	M	A	M	J	J	A	S	O	N	D
°C												
max	2	3	8	13	19	22	25	23	20	13	7	3
min	-3	-3	0	4	8	12	14	13	10	6	2	-1
°F												
max	35	37	46	56	66	72	75	74	68	56	45	38
min	26	26	31	39	47	53	57	56	50	42	36	29

CLOTHING

Pack clothing for the season: heavy coat in winter, light garments and swimwear in summer, raincoat and sweater in spring and autumn.

CRIME AND SAFETY

Berlin is still a very safe city, but like most urban centres, its crime rate is, unfortunately, on the increase. Take the same precautions as you would at home. Report an incident at the nearest police station. The police will give you a certificate to present to your insurance company, or to your consulate if your passport has been stolen.

D

DISABLED TRAVELLERS

Maps of the city transport network show which U- and S-Bahn stations have wheelchair facilities. Buses have wide rear doors and some have lifts and safety straps for wheelchairs. *Berlin Programm* lists which museums cater to visitors with disabilities, although it is always best to phone in advance. For more information, contact the Berlin Tourist Office (see page 129), or call one of the following associations:

Berliner Behindertenverband e.V, tel: 204 38 47

Mobidat, www.mobidat.net.

DRIVING

To enter Germany with your car you will need the following: a national driving licence (or an international licence for those coming from the US, Australia, New Zealand and South Africa); car registration papers; a national identity sticker for your car (except for cars with EU licence plates); a red warning triangle in case of breakdown; and a first-aid kit (the last two items only recommended by law).

Insurance. Third-party insurance is compulsory. Visitors from abroad, except those from EU and certain other European countries, will have to present their international certificate (Green Card) or take out third-party insurance at the border.

Driving conditions. Rush-hour traffic jams and lack of parking space make driving in central Berlin somewhat frustrating. At the beginning and end of peak holiday periods, bottlenecks tend to form on approach roads into Berlin, but traffic generally flows.

Drive on the right, pass on the left. Seat belts are obligatory.

Speed limits. The speed limit in Germany is 100km/h (60mph) on all open roads except motorways and divided highways, where there's no limit unless indicated. (The suggested maximum speed is 130km/h, or 80mph.) In town, speed is restricted to 50km/h (30mph), and often 30km/h (20mph). Cars with trailers may not exceed 80km/h (50mph).

Traffic police may confiscate the car keys of persons they consider unfit to drive. The permissible blood-alcohol level is 0.5 mg per ml.

Breakdowns. For round-the-clock breakdown service call ADAC Auto Assistance, tel: 01802 22 22 22 (without the 01802 dialling code from mobile phones).

Fuel and oil *(Benzin; Öl)*. You'll find petrol stations everywhere, the vast majority of them self-service. Many are open 24 hours.

Umweltzone. Vehicles entering the environmental zone (inside the Berlin S-Bahn ring) must carry a low-emission sticker, which can be obtained from the vehicle registration office or authorized garages (www.berlin.de/umweltzone).

Einbahnstraße one-way street
Fußgänger pedestrians
Kurzparkzone short-term parking
Rechts fahren keep right
Parken verboten no parking
Umleitung detour
Vorsicht caution
driving licence **Führerschein**
car registration papers **Kraftfahrzeugpapiere**
green (insurance) card **Grüne Versicherungskarte**

E

ELECTRICITY

Germany has 220–250 volt, 50-cycle AC. Plugs are the standard continental type, so British and North American devices will need an adaptor. American devices may need a voltage converter.

I need an adaptor/battery, please. **Ich brauche bitte einen Adapter/eine Batterie.**

EMBASSIES AND CONSULATES

Australia: Wallstraße 76–79, 10179 Berlin, tel: 88 00 88.
Canada: Leipziger Platz 17, 10117 Berlin, tel: 20 31 20.

Ireland: Jägerstraße 51, 10117 Berlin, tel: 22 07 20.
South Africa: Tiergartenstraße 18, 10785 Berlin, tel: 22 07 30.
UK: Wilhelmstraße 70–71, 10117 Berlin, tel: 20 45 70.
US: Pariser Platz 2, 10117 Berlin, tel: 23 85 174.

EMERGENCIES (See also Police and Crime and Safety)

The following emergency services are available 24 hours:
Police: **110**
Fire: **112**
Ambulance: **112**
Pharmacies: **0 11 41**
Medical assistance: **31 00 31**
AIDS Hotline: **194 11**

I need a doctor **Ich brauche einen Doktor**
an ambulance **einen Krankenwagen**
a hospital **ein Krankenhaus**

G

GAY AND LESBIAN TRAVELLERS

Berlin has a thriving gay culture, with a massive annual lesbian/gay street festival in early June at Nollendorfplatz and the Christopher Street Day Parade in late June. Most gay venues are around Nollendorfplatz in Schöneberg.

For information about on-going events and related links visit http://berlin.gay-web.de (German-only).

GETTING THERE

By air. There are direct daily flights to Berlin from major airports all over Europe, though travel from the US (except New York) often requires a change of aircraft in Frankfurt or another European city. The cheapest fares on regular flights are available through internet retailers, particularly if you book well in advance. Budget airlines, such as Ryanair, easyJet and Germanwings, offer very low fares if reserved early, but it is worth checking other carriers for better deals. British Airways and Lufthansa fly out of Heathrow to Berlin-Tegel; Air Berlin flies to Berlin-Tegel out of Stansted and Manchester; easyJet operates out of Gatwick, Luton and various UK cities to Berlin-Schönefeld; Ryanair goes to Schönefeld from Stansted and many other British airports. Flights to Berlin's new Brandenburg airport will commmence in 2017.

By rail. Eurostar services from London St Pancras take you to Brussels or Paris, where you can change for trains to Berlin. The best connection is the City Night train from Paris, with a total travel time of 17 hours. It pulls into Hauptbahnhof, Berlin's main station. Daytime trains are faster but require more changes.

By bus. Coaches from London Victoria take about 17 hours to Zentraler Omnibusbahnhof (ZOB) in Berlin.

By road. Berlin is 579 miles/931km from Calais, 446 miles/718km from Hook of Holland, 430miles/692km from Rotterdam and 424 miles/682km from Ijmuiden near Amsterdam. The Harwich-Cuxhaven ferry no longer operates.

GUIDES AND TOURS

If required, the tourist office (BTM) will put you in touch with qualified guides and interpreters for personally conducted tours.

City sightseeing tours by bus are an excellent introduction to Berlin, and most companies offer multilingual recorded commentary. Daily excursions by coach to Potsdam and the Spreewald are also available, as are weekend trips to other places in Germany, including Dresden and Wittenberg.

Most sightseeing tours depart from the Kurfürstendamm, between Rankestraße and Fasanenstraße, but are hop-on hop-off, allowing you to leave and board the bus as often as you want:

Berliner Bären Stadtrundfahrt (BBS), tel: 351 952 70, www.bbs berlin.de. Departs from the Ku'damm at Rankestraße, or can be caught at 15 stops in town.

City-Circle-Tour (Berolina and BVB) departs Ku'damm at Meineckestraße every 15 minutes. You can leave and board the bus at 15 stops.

Top Tour (BVG-Stadttouristik, tel: 256 255 69). Departs from Kurfürstendamm at Café Kranzler every 30 minutes.

Videobustour (Unter den Linden 40, tel: 44 02 44 50, www.videobus tour.de). Film, photos and sound material make this time-travel shuttle an inspiring adventure in history.

Viewing Berlin from the River Spree and the city's canals is a fascinating experience. There's a wide choice of shorter or longer trips, departing from a number of locations including the Nikolaiviertel and Charlottenburger Ufer (near Schloss Charlottenburg).

Reederei Bruno Winkler, tel: 349 95 95

Stern und Kreis Schiffahrt, tel: 536 36 00

There are also a number of very good walking tour operators in the city, the best of which are:

New Berlin Tours, tel: 510 500 30, www.newberlintours.com. Check online for departure times of their daily 3.5-hour free walking tours of Berlin. Only a tip for the English-speaking guide is expected.

Berlin Walks, tel 301 91 94, www.berlinwalks.com.

Insider Tour, tel: 692 31 49, www.insidertour.com.

For a self-guided tour of Berlin focusing on where the Wall was, rent a GPS WallGuide from various locations (see page).

H

HEALTH AND MEDICAL CARE

Take out travel insurance before leaving. Citizens of EU countries may use the German Health Services for medical treatment on presentation of a European Health Insurance Card. This can be applied for at post offices in the UK and Ireland. In the event of accident or serious illness, call for an ambulance, **112**, or ask the medical emergency service, tel: **31 00 31**, to recommend a doctor.

Pharmacies are open during normal shopping hours. They are marked with a red 'A' for Apotheke. At night and on Sundays and holidays, all pharmacies display the address of the nearest open one. Berlin has a special telephone service, Call a Doc (tel: 01805-321 303, www.calladoc.com) that helps you find the right doctor or hospital.

Where's the nearest (all-night) pharmacy? **Wo ist die nächste Apotheke (mit Nachtdienst)?**
What would you recommend for...? **Was empfehlen Sie bei...?**

L

LANGUAGE

Although you can expect many of the people you meet in the west of the city to speak English, this will not necessarily be the case in the east, apart from the 'trendy' areas.

Greet people with *'Guten Tag'* and say goodbye with *'Auf Wiedersehen'*. *'Tschüß'* is a more familiar way of saying goodbye. The word for 'please' is *'bitte'*, also used in the sense of 'you're welcome', and 'thank you' is *'Danke schön'*.

LOST PROPERTY

Berlin's lost-property office (*Zentrales Fundbüro*) is at Platz der Luftbrücke 6 (Tempelhof), tel: 7560-3101. If you left something on public transport, contact the BVG at Potsdamer Straße 180–182 (Schöneberg), tel: 19 449.

M

MAPS

Excellent free street maps *(Stadtplan)* are available at the tourist offices, some car hire agencies and larger hotels.

MEDIA

Major American, British and other European newspapers and magazines are on sale at newsagents, kiosks, big hotels and airports.

It is easy to pick up the BBC World Service. As for television, there are two national channels – ARD and ZDF – plus a regional station, RBB. CNN and BBC News are probably all you will find in English.

MONEY

Currency. Euro (EUR/€) notes are denominated in 5, 10, 20, 50, 100 and 500 euros; coins in 1 and 2 euros and 1, 2, 5, 10, 20 and 50 cents.
Changing money. The easiest way to obtain euros is at an ATM machine. Foreign currency can be changed at ordinary banks *(Bank)*, savings banks *(Sparkasse)*, and currency exchange offices *(Wechselstube)*. Hotels, travel agencies, and the central post office also have exchange facilities, but rates are less favourable.

I want to change some pounds/dollars. **Ich möchte Pfund/ Dollar wechseln**.
Can you cash a traveller's cheque? **Können sie einen Reisescheck einlösen**?
Where's the nearest bank/currency exchange office? **Wo ist die nächste Bank/Wechselstube**?
Is there a cash machine near here? **Gibt es hier einen Geldautomaten?**
How much is that? **Wieviel kostet das?**

O

OPENING TIMES

Department stores are open Monday–Saturday 10am–8pm. Smaller shops may not open until around 10am and close early on Saturday. A few supermarkets in or around railway stations are open on Sunday.

Banking hours are usually Mon–Fri 9am–3pm. Most banks remain open one or more afternoons a week; however days vary. The currency exchange office of the ReiseBank in the Hauptbahnhof is open daily 8am–10pm. Most museums in Berlin are closed on Monday.

P

POLICE

Germany's police officers wear dark blue uniforms. You'll see them on white motorcycles or in blue-and-silver cars or vans. The police emergency number is **110**.

Where's the nearest police station? **Wo ist die nächste Polizeistation?**
I've lost my... **Ich habe...**
wallet/bag/passport. **meine brieftasche/meine tasche/ meinen reisepass verloren.**

POST OFFICES

Postboxes are bright yellow and, if there is more than one slot on a mail box, you should deposit non-local letters or cards in the slot marked *Andere* PLZ.

The post office at Flughafen Tegel (airport) is open Monday–Friday 8am–6pm, and Saturday 8am–1pm. The self-service area is open 24 hours. The branch at Hauptbahnhof is open Mon–Fri 7am–10pm, Sat–Sun 8am–10pm. Information on other postal services can be found at: www.deutschepost.de.

Where's the nearest post office? **Wo ist das nächste Postamt?**
express (special delivery) **per Eilboten**
registered **per Einschreiben**

PUBLIC HOLIDAYS

The chart below shows the public holidays celebrated in Berlin when shops, banks, official departments and many restaurants are closed.

On 24 December (Christmas Eve), shops stay open until noon, but most restaurants, theatres, cinemas and concert halls are closed.

1 January **Neujahr** New Year's Day
1 May **Tag der Arbeit** Labour Day
3 October **Tag der Deutschen Einheit** Reunification Day
25, 26 December **Weihnachten** Christmas
Movable dates:
Karfreitag Good Friday
Ostermontag Easter Monday
Christi Himmelfahrt Ascension Day
Pfingstmontag Whit Monday

T

TELEPHONES

The dialling code for Germany is 49. The dialling code for Berlin from outside the city is 030. Drop the first zero when calling from outside the country.

Although some phone booths are still coin-operated, those accepting phone cards *(telefonkarte)* are more common, and there are some that also accept credit cards. Phone cards can be obtained at any post office and many kiosks. Communications within Germany and to neighbouring countries are cheaper weekdays 6pm–8am and all day Saturday–Sunday. Rates for Canada and the US are lower midnight–noon.

Enquiries: domestic, tel: 11 8 33; international, tel: 11 8 34.

TIME ZONES

Germany follows Central European Time (GMT +1) and daylight saving time changes take place on the same days as in the UK:

New York	London	**Berlin**	Jo'burg	Sydney	Auckland
6am	11am	**noon**	noon	8pm	10pm

TIPPING

Since a service charge is normally included in hotel and restaurant bills, tipping is not obligatory, although it is gladly accepted.

TOILETS

Herren indicates Gentlemen and *Damen* indicates Ladies.

Where are the toilets? **Wo sind die Toiletten?**

TOURIST INFORMATION

The headquarter of the German National Tourist Board – Deutsche Zentrale für Tourismus e.V. (DZT) – is located at: Beethovenstraße 69, D-60325 Frankfurt am Main, tel: (069) 97 46 40.

The German National Tourist Board also maintains offices in many countries throughout the world:

Canada: 2 Bloor Street West, Suite 2601, Toronto, ON, M4W 3E2, tel: +1 416 935 1896 ext. 224

UK: 60 Buckingham Palace Road, London SW1W 0AH, tel + 44 (0)207 3170 914

US: 122 East 42nd Street, New York, NY 10168-0072, tel: (212) 661-7200; 1334 Parkview Avenue, Suite 300, Manhattan Beach, CA 90266, tel: (310) 545-1350

The Berlin Tourist Office, Berlin Tourismus Marketing GmbH (www.visitberlin.de; Berlin Hotline tel: 25 00 23 33), runs a number of **information points** in the city.

Brandenburger Tor, South Wing; daily 9.30am–7pm.

Fernsehturm, Panoramastraße 1a; daily 10am–6pm.

Hauptbahnhof (Central Station), Floor 0/Entrance North, Europa Platz 1; daily 8am–10pm.

Neues Kranzler Eck, Passage, Kurfürstendamm 22, Mon–Sat 9.30am–8pm, Sun 10am–6pm.

Some information points operate longer opening hours Apr–Oct. There are also tourist information points at both airports.

In addition to free maps, lists and brochures, Berlin's tourist offices sell the Welcome Card (see page 130) and museum tickets; tickets for the theatre and other events can also be purchased.

TRANSPORT

Berlin is served by an efficient network of buses, trams, U-Bahn (underground railway), S-Bahn (suburban railway), and Regionalbahn (regional railway), administered by the *Berliner Verkehrsbetriebe*, or BVG for short. The U-Bahn currently covers the inner city and many outlying districts, while the bus service reaches nearly every corner of Berlin. The S-Bahn (administrated by Deutsche Bahn) provides an efficient link to places further afield such as the Grunewald, Wannsee, Potsdam and Köpenick, and its central, overhead section linking Savignyplatz, Zoologischer Garten, Friedrichstraße and Alexanderplatz is particularly useful. The tram network operates mainly in the former East Berlin.

The **U-Bahn** operates Sunday–Thursday 4.30am–1am; Friday–

Saturday most lines run all night. U-Bahn stations are marked by a white 'U' on a blue background, and S-Bahn stations by a white 'S' on a green background.

Buses and **trams** run at least 20 hours a day at 10-minute intervals (every 20–30 minutes at night). Night bus routes coincide with the U-Bahn network. Bus stops are easily recognisable by a yellow sign marked with a green 'H'.

> When's the next bus to...? **Wann geht der nächste Bus nach...?**
>
> Will you tell me when to get off? **Könnten Sie mir bitte sagen, wann ich aussteigen muss.**

Tickets are interchangeable between trains, buses and trams, entitling you to free transfers for up to two hours (no return allowed). Be sure to have plenty of small change for the ticket machines at the U-Bahn stations and most bus stops. A few of them also take banknotes. Stamp your ticket at the start of your journey in one of the red or yellow machines (*entwerter*) on station platforms and in buses. You can also buy a ticket on the bus itself. The most cost-effective option is to buy either a one-day ticket (*tageskarte*, €6.70 or €7.20 for two or three zones), or a one-day group ticket (*kleingruppenkarte*, €16.20 for up to five people). They both allow travel up to 3am the day after the ticket is stamped at an *entwerter*, and the group ticket covers up to five people.

Holders of the **Welcome Card**, which is available from Tourist Offices, S-Bahn ticket offices, BVG ticket offices and many hotels for €36.50 (zones A, B, and C) or €31.50 (A and B), are entitled to 72 hours of unlimited use of public transport throughout the city, in addition to reduced entry prices for many of the city's major museums and attractions. A seven-day ticket (public transport only) costs €28.80 (A and B) or €35.60 (A, B and C). Zone A covers the inner city including the S-Bahn ring, zone B stretches to the city limits and zone C includes the suburbs, Potsdam and Schönefeld airport.

Deutsche Bahn (German Rail) trains are comfortable and fast. EC (EuroCity) are international trains; IC (InterCity) and ICE (Inter City Express) are long-distance national trains. First-class travel on the Deutsche Bahn costs double the second-class fare. A supplement is charged for travel on EuroCity, ICE and InterCity trains. Children under 4 travel free in Germany, while 4–12 year-olds pay half fare.

There are several travel passes, including the German Rail pass, which allow unlimited travel in Germany for any three to eight days within one month. Detailed information is available, in English, from the Deutsche Bahn website www.bahn.de or the Deutsche Bahn UK Booking Centre in England, tel: (+44) (0)871 880 80 66 (open Mon–Fri 9am–8pm, Sat–Sun 9am–1pm).

Long-distance buses depart from the central bus station (Zentral Omnibus Bahnhof Funkturm, ZOB) near the Funkturm (radio tower) in Messedamm, tel: 302 53 61.

Berlin **taxis** are mostly cream-coloured Mercedes. You can book in advance through your hotel, or tel: 0800 222 22 55.

Velo Taxis are bicycle-powered rickshaws, found in busy tourist areas (tel: 0178 80 000 41; www.velotaxi.com).

Where can I get a taxi? **Wo finde ich ein Taxi?**

V

VISAS AND ENTRY REQUIREMENTS

Visitors from EU countries only need a national ID card (or passport) to enter Germany. Citizens of most other countries, including the US, Canada, Australia and New Zealand, must have a valid passport. Residents of South Africa need a visa to enter Germany.

W

WEBSITES AND INTERNET ACCESS

Some useful addresses:

www.bahn.de Deutsche Bahn website.

www.berlin.de Official site of the state of Berlin.

www.berlinonline.de German-language listings and news site.

www.visitberlin.de Official tourism website.

www.smb.museum Site for all the state museums in Berlin.

http://berlin.angloinfo.com District-by-district *What's On* guide.

www.cafespots.de List of free Wi-fi hotspots in Berlin.

Y

YOUTH HOSTELS

The local branch of the German Youth Hostel Association (DJH Landesverband Berlin-Brandenburg) is at Tempelhofer Ufer 32, 10963 Berlin, tel: 26 49 52 0, www.djh-berlin-brandenburg.de. Youth hostels tend to get crowded, so you should always book ahead.

Berlin International Youth Hostel, Kluckstraße 3, 10785 Berlin, tel: 74 76 87 91 0; www.jh-berlin-international.de. Dorm from €17.

Jugendgästehaus Am Wannsee, Badeweg 1, 14129 Berlin, tel: 803 20 34; www.jh-wannsee.de . B&B €17.

Jugendherberge Ernst Reuter, Hermsdorfer Damm 48–50, 13467 Berlin, tel: 404 16 10; www.jh-ernst-reuter.de. B&B €17.

The A&O hostels are centrally located, have dormitories and private rooms, and friendly staff; www.aohostels.com. €7–25 per person.

RECOMMENDED HOTELS

If you are coming to Berlin for a trade fair, convention, or want to enjoy the old-world elegant charm of a bourgeois neighbourhood, the West Berlin/Charlottenburg area is probably for you. Hotels in Mitte, in former East Berlin, are typically more recently built or converted: some of them are modern and very stylish, and much closer to the famous Museum Island, Potsdamer Platz and the historic city centre.

The less central areas of Mitte and Prenzlauer Berg offer more affordable accommodation, plenty of nightlife and more opportunities to mix with the locals.

If you prefer a peaceful location, you might consider Spandau or the Grunewald. Alternatively, you can stay in one of Potsdam's charming hotels, close to the palaces and gardens, and only about an hour away from Berlin.

As a basic guide to prices, we have used the following symbols (for an en-suite double room and usually breakfast):

€€€€	above €250
€€€	€150–250
€€	€80–150
€	below €80

BERLIN

BERLIN CITY, WEST

Artemisia €€ *Brandenburgische Straße 18, 10707 Berlin, tel: 860 93 20*, www.hotel-artemisia.de. Simple but spotless rooms in a perfect location and serving up a very good breakfast. 19 rooms and a cosy sun deck.

Askanischer Hof €€ *Kurfürstendamm 53, 10707 Berlin, tel: 881 80 33*, www.askanischer-hof.de. A small, family-run hotel with 16 rooms in an excellent location. Delightful, authentic 1920s atmosphere and a very friendly reception. Children welcome.

Astoria am Kurfürstendamm €€ *Fasanenstraße 2, 10623 Berlin, tel: 312 40 67*. Very friendly 19th-century townhouse hotel in an agreeable central location just off the Kurfürstendamm. Special rates are available for children under 12. Babysitting facilities. 32 rooms.

The Ellington Hotel Berlin €€€€ *Nürnberger Straße 50–55, 10789 Berlin, tel: 68 31 50*, www.ellington-hotel.com. This 285-room hotel is housed in a magnificent building that conserves the architectural style of the golden twenties and offers high-quality elegance, professional service and a lively atmosphere. It also hosts the world's biggest Elvis exhibition, from photographs to his stage costumes.

Grand Hotel Esplanade €€€€ *Lützowufer 15, 10785 Berlin, tel: 25 47 80*, www.esplanade.de. This 'lifestyle' hotel features sleek and creative interior design and 394 rooms. Harry's New York Bar on the ground floor is one of the best addresses for long drinks in Berlin.

Hotel-Pension Funk €€ *Fasanenstraße 69, 10719 Berlin, tel: 882 71 93*, www.hotel-pensionfunk.de. This small, 14-room hotel has comfortable rooms, though not all have showers. Located in one of the most delightful streets off the busy Kurfürstendamm, this Art Nouveau building was once home to a silent screen star.

Hotel Q! €€€ *Knesebeckstraße 67, 10623 Berlin, tel: 810 06 60*, www. hotel-q.com. This establishment on the corner of the Ku'damm takes the concept of the design hotel to its limits, with never a right angle in sight and a pervasive sense of playfulness. A unique experience. Very special bar.

Kempinski Hotel Bristol €€€€ *Kurfürstendamm 27, 10719 Berlin, tel: 88 43 40*, www.kempinskiberlin.de. Large, luxurious hotel with excellent facilities: conference rooms, several restaurants, solarium, sauna, babysitting services, indoor swimming pool. The soundproofed rooms are extremely comfortable and pleasantly furnished. Disabled access. 301 rooms.

Lindner Hotel am Ku'damm €€€ *Kurfürstendamm 24, 10719 Berlin, tel: 818 250*, www.lindner.de. Part of the City Quartier development at Kranzler Eck, the Lindner has 124 comfortable and spacious rooms with state-of-the-art communications facilities. The Outlook restaurant, with its pleasant courtyard, serves light 21st-century dishes; there is a sauna and sun deck; and the Fitness First Black Label Berlin next door at the Neues Kranzler Eck complex offers a wide range of fitness facilities.

Mondial €€€ *Kurfürstendamm 47, 10707 Berlin, tel: 88 41 10*, www.hotel-mondial.com. Comfortable rooms and friendly service are just two of this hotel's assets. Excellent facilities for disabled visitors. Restaurant and bar, conference rooms, wellness area, and parking all come as part of the deal. 75 rooms.

NH Berlin Kurfürstendamm €€€ *Grolmanstraße 41–43, 10623 Berlin, tel: 88 42 60*, www.nh-hotels.com. In a quiet location near Savignyplatz, this elegant hotel offers 167 tastefully furnished rooms, as well as a sauna and solarium, restaurant with garden terrace and bar.

Schlossparkhotel €€€ *Heubnerweg 2a, 14059 Berlin, tel: 326 90 30*, www.schlossparkhotel.de. Situated in a quiet location near Charlottenburg Palace gardens, this 32-room hotel has a swimming pool as well as conference facilities.

Hotel Seehof am Lietzensee €€€ *Lietzensee-Ufer 11, 14057 Berlin, tel: 32 00 20*, www.hotel-seehof-berlin.de. Modern hotel on the shores of a little lake in one of the city's most exclusive residential areas. A restaurant, swimming pool, solarium, sauna and Ayurveda treatments are just some of the extras on offer. The 75 generously sized rooms are traditionally decorated and many enjoy wonderful views of the lake.

POTSDAMER PLATZ/KREUZBERG

Berlin Marriott €€€€ *Inge-Beisheim-Platz 1, 10785 Berlin, tel: 22 00 00*, www.marriott.com. Part of the prestigious Beisheim Center on Potsdamer Platz. Has all of the usual Marriott facilities, 379 rooms and suites, and an executive floor.

Grand Hyatt Berlin €€€€ *Marlene-Dietrich-Platz 2, 10785 Berlin, tel: 25 53 12 34*, www.hyatt.de. Very up-to-the-minute hotel, located right on Potsdamer Platz, opposite the Musical Theatre. It is also within easy walking distance of the Kulturforum. Has 342 rooms, a swimming pool, gym and disabled access.

Riehmers Hofgarten €€ *Yorckstraße 83, 10965 Berlin, tel: 78 09 88 00*, www.riehmers-hofgarten.de. Comfy digs in a charming historic building near leafy Viktoria Park, with restaurant and conference facilities. The hotel is well situated for exploring Kreuzberg and Mitte. 22 rooms.

Ritz-Carlton Berlin €€€€ *Potsdamer Platz 3, 10785 Berlin, tel: 33 77 77*, www.ritzcarlton.com/hotels/berlin. The last word in luxury and style occupying the main Chicago-style Beisheim Center building overlooking Potsdamer Platz. Interior design inspired by Karl Friedrich Schinkel. Top-notch service as you might expect at these prices. 343 rooms including luxury suites.

BERLIN CITY, EAST

Adlon Kempinski €€€€ *Unter den Linden 77, 10117 Berlin, tel: 22 610*, www.kempinski.com. The original Hotel Adlon was a Berlin legend that welcomed such luminaries as Charlie Chaplin and Greta Garbo. It was destroyed in 1945 so what you see today is the new Adlon built in 1997. The hotel has remained true to the traditions of its famous predecessor, boasting the very best of everything in one of the world's top hotels, including a Michelin-starred restaurant, Lorenz Adlon. The black marble elephant fountain in the hall once stood in the original Hotel Adlon. 382 rooms including suites.

art'otel Berlin Mitte €€€ *Wallstraße 70–73; 10179 Berlin, tel: 24 06 20*, www.artotels.com. Elegant hotel with a mixture of classical and modern architecture and contemporary art and design. It has 109 rooms and a stylish restaurant, the Factory.

Circus Hotel €€ *Rosenthalerstraße 1; 10119 Berlin, tel: 20 00 39 39*, www.circus-berlin.de. Green boutique hotel with design-conscious room decor and a list of extras as long as the Wall once was (bike hire, rickshaw tours, yoga classes). The organic buffet breakfast costs an extra €9. Has 62 rooms.

The Dude €€€ *Köpenicker Straße 92; 10179 Berlin, tel: 411 988 177*, www.thedudeberlin.com. Quirky boutique hotel with a spiral Schinkel staircase climbing to 30 immaculately designed chambers, each containing handpicked furniture and fittings that will certainly inspire you to change that old sofa back home. Breakfast is extra and is served in the downstairs deli.

H2 Hotel Berlin Alexanderplatz € *Karl-Liebknecht-Straße 32, 10178 Berlin, tel: 24 08 80 10*, www.h2-hotels.de. Minimalist budget hotel with 288 immaculately kept no-frills rooms. If you're looking for lots of extras, go elsewhere and breakfasts can become monotonous if staying more than a few days. But overall amazing value for money for this location.

Hilton Berlin €€€€ *Mohrenstraße 30, 10117 Berlin, tel: 202 300*, www. berlin.hilton.com. Big modern hotel on the historic Gendarmenmarkt square. Offers 589 excellent rooms as well as two restaurants, a bistro, a café and a pub. Sports facilities include a sauna, swimming pool and squash court. Disabled access.

Honigmond Hotel and Garden Hotel €€€ *Tieckstraße 11 and Invalidenstraße 122, 10115 Berlin, tel: 28 44 550/28 44 5577*, www. honigmond.de. Fabulous 60-room family hotel. Two charming old buildings on the same block, with large, beautifully appointed rooms, plus bar and excellent restaurant. Friedrichstraße and Oranienburger Straße are within walking distance or a couple of stops by tram.

Michalberger Hotel €€ *Warschauer Straße 39-40, 10243 Berlin, tel: 29 77 85 90*, www.michelbergerhotel.com. Located in Friedrichshain on the eastern fringes of the city centre, this superb, hip hotel offers stylish accommodation for budget prices. The lounge is where travellers from across the globe meet up and there's a great restaurant serving tasty fare. If you are looking for Berlin's quirky, alternative side, this is a good place to stay. 119 rooms.

Motel One Berlin-Alexanderplatz € *Dircksenstraße 36, 10179 Berlin, tel: 20 05 40 80*, www.motel-one.de. Definitely the lodgings of choice for those who care more about location than style and hotel extras. Sleep, shower and surf the web all a short walk away from the city's sights. The chain has eight other equally affordable hotels to choose from across the city. 207 rooms.

Park Inn €€€ *Alexanderplatz 7, 10178 Berlin, tel: 23 890,* www.park inn.com. The 37-storey hotel, with a whopping 1,012 rooms, offers stunning views from its rooms and elegant interiors, though the bedrooms are generally on the small side.

Radisson Blu Hotel Berlin €€€ *Karl-Liebknecht-Straße 3, 10178 Berlin, tel: 23 82 80,* www.radissonblu.com/hotel-berlin. Contemporary, 427-room hotel located close to the Berliner Dom and Museumsinsel. Its lobby holds the world's largest cylindrical aquarium, a truly spectacular sight. Stocked with 2,500 exotic tropical fish, the AquaDom is 25m (80ft) high and part of the adjoining Sea Life Berlin. Facilities include four restaurants, sauna, conference centre and bar.

The Regent €€€€ *Charlottenstraße 49, 10117 Berlin, tel: 20 338,* www. regenthotels.com. Sumptuously decorated hotel in the historic heart of Berlin, directly across from the Gendarmenmarkt. The staff here are exceptionally well trained. 195 rooms.

Hotel de Rome €€€€ *Behrenstraße 37, 10117 Berlin, tel: 460 60 90,* www.roccofortehotels.com. This luxury hotel on Bebelplatz, next to the Staatsoper Unter den Linden, is located in a building dating back to 1889 that housed the head office of Dresdner Bank until 1945. The ornate and classical design of the bank has been given a contemporary twist. The bank vault is now a 20-metre (66ft) -long swimming pool surrounded by a spa. The restaurant looks onto a large external terrace and offers alfresco dining during the summer. 146 rooms.

Hotel Transit Loft €€ *Immanuelkirchstraße 14a, 10405 Berlin-Prenzlauer Berg, tel: 484 937 73,* www.transit-loft.de. Modern hostel/hotel in a converted 19th-century factory building in the heart of hip Prenzlauer Berg. The 47 rooms (1–5 beds) are bright and functionally furnished, ideal for families with children and groups. All are ensuite, with a shower and toilet.

The Westin Grand Berlin €€€€ *Friedrichstraße 158–64, Berlin 10117, tel: 202 70*, www.westingrandberlin.com. This elegantly decorated hotel at the corner of Friedrichstraße and Unter den Linden has 400 rooms and suites, excellent restaurants, a beautiful garden and top spa services.

OUTSKIRTS

Hotel Maison Apartments am Kolk €€ *Kolk 10, 13597 Berlin, tel: 841 139 10*, www.aparthotel-amkolk.de. Eight charming furnished apartments with Wi-fi in the neighbourhood of Spandau, with a weekly market and beer gardens overlooking the river Havel nearby. A short walk away, the subway gets you to central Berlin in 20 minutes. Better suited for longer stays, since there is an end-of-stay cleaning charge.

Schlosshotel im Grunewald €€€€ *Brahmsstraße 10, 14193 Berlin, tel: 895 840*, www.schlosshotelberlin.com. Luxurious elegance in an historic mansion set in a private park, with interior design by the illustrious Karl Lagerfeld. Excellent leisure facilities, including sauna, solarium and swimming pool. Good restaurant and 53 rooms.

POTSDAM

arcona Hotel Am Havelufer €€€ *Zeppelinstraße 136, 14471 Potsdam, tel: (0331) 98 150*, www.potsdam.arcona.de. A stunning hotel situated on the banks of the Havel River. The building is a combination of a beautifully restored 19th-century granary and some striking modern architecture. Facilities include Wi-fi, sauna, solarium and fitness area. 123 rooms and suites.

Schlosshotel Cecilienhof €€€€ *Neuer Garten, 14469 Potsdam, tel: (0331) 3 70 50*, www.relexa-hotels.de. English-style, half-timbered country house built for the Kaiser's son, Crown Prince Wilhelm (see page). This unique, 42-room establishment is linked to the centre of Potsdam by bus or lovely lakeside footpath. A favourite with visiting heads of state. Closed for renovation until 2018.

INDEX

INSIGHT ⊙ GUIDES POCKET GUIDE

BERLIN

First Edition 2016
Written by Brigitte Lee, Jack Messenger and
Jack Altman
Updated by Magdalena Helsztyńska-Stadnik
Update Production: AM Services
Edited by Kate Drynan
Maps updated by Carte Warsaw
Photography credits: Apa Publications 2BR, 3BL,
17, 19; AWL Images Ltd 30; Berlin Tourismus
Marketing (BTM)/Koch 2MC, 51, 71, 77, 87;
Chris Coe/Apa Publications 2TL, 3ML, 3MR,
3TR, 6TL, 35, 37, 39, 64, 65, 73, 84, 88; Corbis
20; Getty Images 23, 25, 26, 46; Glyn Genin/
Apa Publications 2TR, 4ML, 4MR, 4TL, 4BL, 5BM, 5TL,
5TR, 6BR, 6ML, 7TR, 7 BR, 12, 43, 55, 59, 75, 81,
92, 100, 104; Operncafé on Unter den Linden 4TR,
99; Tony Halliday/Apa Publications 2DL, 3DR,
3TL, 4BL, 7MC, 11, 13, 15, 32, 36, 41, 44, 47, 49,
52, 56, 61, 63, 66, 69, 79, 83, 91, 94, 95
Cover picture: iStock
All Rights Reserved
© 2016 Apa Digital (CH) AC and
Apa Publications (UK) Ltd

Distribution

UK, Ireland and Europe: Apa Publications (UK)
Ltd; sales@insightguides.com
United States and Canada: Ingram Publisher
Services; ips@ingramcontent.com

Australia and New Zealand: Woodslane;
info@woodslane.com.au
Southeast Asia: Apa Publications (SN) Pte;
singaporeoffice@insightguides.com
Hong Kong, Taiwan and China:
Apa Publications (HK) Ltd;
hongkongoffice@insightguides.com
Worldwide: Apa Publications (UK) Ltd;
sales@insightguides.com

**Special Sales, Content Licensing
and CoPublishing**
Insight Guides can be purchased in bulk quan-
tities at discounted prices. We can create special
editions, personalised jackets and corporate
imprints tailored to your needs. sales@insight
guides.com; www.insightguides.biz

Printed in Poland

No part of this book may be reproduced, stored
in a retrieval system or transmitted in any form
or means mechanical, photocopying,
recording or otherwise, without prior written
permission from Apa Publications.

Contact us
Every effort has been made to provide accurate
information in this publication, but changes are
inevitable. The publisher cannot be responsible
for any resulting loss, inconvenience or injury.
We would appreciate it if readers would call our
attention to any errors or outdated information.
We also welcome your suggestions; please
contact us at: hello@insightguides.com
www.insightguides.com

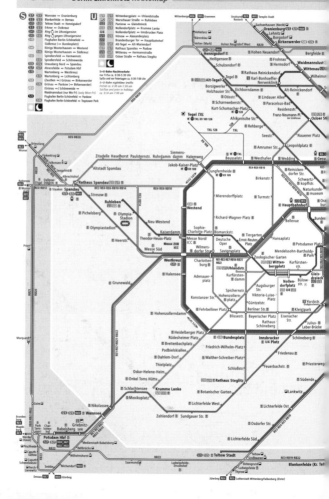

SU Berlin Liniennetz *Routemap*